NOTE: Before you jump in with this QR Code, make sure you've read The Newspotent YearBook, 2024 completely!

This special edition brings together the most exciting and important stories from The Newspotent newspapers for the Academic Year **2024-25**.

From **news, science, and sports to puzzles, roleplay, and inspiring stories,** it's all here!

Every Question in the Test is Picked Straight from this- The Newspotent YearBook, 2024!

JUNE

EDIT

'CUP OF JOY': INDIA LIFTS T20 WORLD CUP AFTER 17 YEARS

India finally ended its long wait to get its hands on another T20 World Cup by beating first-time finalists South Africa by seven runs in a nail-biting final at the Kensington Oval in Barbados on **June 29, 2024.**

With this remarkable feat, India joined the West Indies and England as the only teams to have won the Men's T20 World Cup twice.

The 'Player of the Match' Virat Kohli's impressive 76-run contribution in the first innings powered India's total to 176, the highest score ever in a T20 World Cup final.

Kohli is the only player in the history of cricket to win the U-19 World Cup (2008), the ODI World Cup (2011), the Champions Trophy (2013) and the T20 World Cup (2024).

Jasprit Bumrah was named "Player of the Tournament" for his outstanding bowling performance in the T20 World Cup (15 wickets); he picked 2 wickets for 18 runs in the final.

The winning team, India, received $2.45 million (20.42 crore INR), and South Africa, the runners-up, bagged $1.28 million (10.6 crore INR) in prize money from the ICC. The victorious Indian team would also get Rs. 125 crore from the BCCI.

However, this victory ended on an emotional note for Indian cricket fans as legendary Indian batter Virat Kohli announced his retirement from the T20I (Twenty 20 International) format: "This was my last T20 World Cup... Time for the next generation to take the T20 game forward." Following Kohli's retirement, India's skipper Rohit Sharma, and all-rounder Ravinder Jadeja also announced retirement.

ISRAELI COMPANY SETS UP FIRST WIRELESS EV CHARGING ROAD IN NORWAY

Norway installed its first wireless charging road on **June 30, 2024,** allowing electric vehicles to charge while in motion.

Special copper coils connected to the electricity grid are placed beneath the road surface in these EV charging roads, also called the wireless Electric Road System (ERS).

Electric cars, or EVs, are continually charged as they travel along the ERS due to a unique receiver installed in the car and connected to the battery.

A year-long test will be held using four electric buses on a long road in Trondheim. **During this test, the technology's capacity to operate buses continuously throughout the day without stopping to charge will be proven.**

This project will cost around 22.4 million Norwegian kroner (NOK), funded by the government.

[1 million = 10 lakh, 1 NOK = Rs. 7.50 (as of Dec 31, 2024)]

PROVERBS & PHRASES

'Worth its weight in gold'

Meaning: To be very useful or helpful.

Example: This book on Kashmir is worth its weight in gold; it has everything you need to know about the place.

MATH PUZZLE

The length and breadth of a rectangular field are 600 m and 400 m respectively. Find the cost of the grass to be planted in it at the rate of ₹ 2.50 per square metres.

HOW TO BE CREATIVE ?

Do you believe that human creativity might eventually be replaced by artificial intelligence? Provide reasons supporting or refuting the assertion.

HISTORIC! CHINA'S CHANG'E-6 RETURNS WITH FIRST-EVER SAMPLE FROM MOON'S FAR SIDE

China's Chang'e-6 lunar probe (crewless spacecraft) safely brought back the first samples from the moon's far side to Earth. The spacecraft landed in Inner Mongolia on **June 25, 2024.**

The South Pole-Aitken basin is one of the oldest and biggest craters on the moon. The spacecraft's lander used a robotic arm and drill to gather rock and soil from the basin for two days. The US, China, and the former Soviet Union have all obtained specimens from the near side of the moon, but China is the first nation to obtain samples from the far side.

Investigating the samples from the far side will help scientists understand the moon's formation and history.

The far side of the moon is commonly referred to as the "dark side," as it cannot be seen from Earth.

SUNIL CHHETRI BID FAREWELL TO INTERNATIONAL FOOTBALL; TEAMMATES GAVE TEARFUL 'GUARD OF HONOUR'

Sunil Chhetri's nearly two-decade-long, spectacular international football career ended on **June 6, 2024,** at Kolkata's famed Salt Lake Stadium as he wore the national jersey for his final international match against Kuwait. India had to win this match against Kuwait to qualify for the next stage of the FIFA World Cup, but regrettably, the result was a tie.

"I've been fighting a small battle every day. Don't ask me how I feel (about retirement). Because I don't want to address it. We really need to win.." Chhetri shared before the crucial clash. Chhetri's life has always been all about football.

Beginning his career in 2002, he went on to become India's all-time best goal scorer and the fourth-highest international goalscorer.

Chhetri's outstanding performance helped India win the SAFF Championship in 2011, 2015, 2021, and 2023.

Chhetri, who was named 'Player of the Year' by the All India Football Federation a record seven times, was honoured with the Arjuna Award in 2011 for his exceptional athletic accomplishment and the Padma Shri award, India's fourth-highest civilian honour, in 2019. **He became the first football player to win India's highest sports distinction, the Khel Ratna Award, in 2021.**

IMAGE DECODER

PM MODI 'S "MANN KI BAAT" RESUMES AFTER THREE MONTHS, HIGHLIGHTING #PLANT4MOTHER CAMPAIGN

Here are a few points that PM Modi covered on the 111th episode (**aired on June 30**) of the 'Mann Ki Baat' address:

Referring to the "#ek_paid_maa_ke_naam" (#PLANT4MOTHER) campaign, **the prime minister discussed the sacrifices made by mothers in raising their children. He encouraged people to plant a tree in honour of their mothers as a means of acknowledging their "unpayable debt to her."**

He encouraged people to share their picture of planting a tree with their mother or her picture as a mark of respect for her and Mother Earth.

PM Modi mentioned that Turkmenistan celebrated the 300th birthday of its national poet in May by unveiling statues of 24 renowned poets from around the world, including Indian Nobel laureate Rabindranath Tagore.

ROLE PLAY - VOCABULARY

Student 1: You appear disoriented. Are you feeling sad for any reason?

Student 2: I spotted a little girl, maybe 6 or 7 years old, selling balloons at the signal on my way to school today. Despite my strong desire to help her, I was unable to do anything. I wish she could also go to school like us.

Student 1: It may sound harsh, but for someone who can't even afford two meals a day, attending school is no less than an extravagance.

Student 2: Can't we do something for them?

Student 1: I think we can. We can visit adjoining slums on Saturdays to help impoverished girls like her learn the fundamentals of education. Let's request that our class teacher acquire Principal Mam's authorization.

Student 2: Yeah, let's also talk about this with our peers to see how many of them are up for this commendable effort.

Dictionary

Disoriented: To feel lost or confused.

Extravagance: Excessive or unnecessary expenditure

Impoverished: Poor

Commendable: Praiseworthy

MATHS CROSSWORD.............

12	+		=	36				
		÷		÷				+
	−		=	4				23
×		=		=		÷		=
		6			×	5	=	
=						=		
56		20	−		=	11		3
		+		×				×
84	÷		=					13
		=		=				=
				63	−		=	

ON THIS DAY OF JUNE 14:

In 1949, Albert II, a monkey, rode a V-2 rocket to an altitude of 134 km, thereby becoming the first mammal and first monkey in space.

'I HAVEN'T GOT TO MY PEAK YET': OLYMPIC CHAMPION NEERAJ CHOPRA

Neeraj Chopra, the 26-year-old athlete who became the first Indian to win gold in the javelin at the Olympics and the World Championship, clarified that he is yet to achieve his best performance.

"To date, I am only satisfied with one throw of mine, which was 86.48 m in the World Under-20 Championships 2016. That was one throw that I felt was a special, unique one, but I have not been satisfied with any throw since," the athlete revealed on **June 14, 2024.**

"I have many hobbies. I like hanging out with my friends. I also liked shopping a lot, but now I shop less because it feels like a waste of money. We can spend that money elsewhere. I like collecting unique things. I once went past a shop in Germany that had unique art pieces. I liked a statue of a warrior sitting on a horse, throwing a spear—more like throwing a javelin—so I bought it without even thinking. It was 20 kg," the 2023 World Champion shared on JioCinema's 'Get Set Gold.'

"I watched movies with the best IMDb ratings… *'The Shawshank Redemption,' 'Forrest Gump,' 'A Beautiful Mind,'* and *'The Pianist.'* I recently watched the movie *'Society of the Snow.'* I would like to tell everyone to watch it. It makes me feel like our lives are much better," the athlete remarked.

"I don't have a favourite playlist but during events, I mostly listen to loud music… Once I was competing in the Asian Games, and I listened to Shiv Tandav; it gave me goosebumps. I like adrenaline-pumping music because.. when I compete, I get very aggressive," Neeraj disclosed.

WHO AM I?

1. I am an Indian professional tennis player who specialises in doubles.
2. After winning my first major doubles title at the 2024 Australian Open, I became the oldest first-time No. 1 at 43.
3. I have also won 26 doubles titles on the ATP Tour, including six at the Masters 1000 level, with a title at the 2023 Indian Wells Masters, making me the oldest Masters winner. (ATP: Association of Tennis Professionals)
4. I was a recipient of the Arjuna Award, the second-highest sporting honour in India, in 2019.

VERBAL ROLEPLAY

Student 1: What summertime activities have you planned?

Student 2: I have decided to master something new this summer.

Student 1: That's nice. What are you planning to take up?

Student 2: I am not proficient in swimming; hence, I intend to join some swimming classes to acquire the required expertise.

Student 1: Wow, I have heard swimming helps build endurance, muscle strength and cardiovascular fitness. Do you mind if I sign up for the swimming class with you?

Student 2: That's an awesome idea. Having your company during the swimming lessons would be delightful.

Dictionary

Endurance: It refers to a person's capability to continue an exercise or physical activity for a long time.

Proficient: Good at doing something, especially through practice.

Acquire: To gain something through your own efforts.

Delightful: Enjoyable

LEGENDARY ACTOR NANA PATEKAR RECALLS SERVING INDIA IN THE KARGIL WAR

Veteran actor Nana Patekar disclosed in an interview on **June 23, 2024**, that he participated in the Kargil War: "I was a member of the Quick Reaction Team. It is one of the most elite forces."

Quick Reaction Teams are trained to handle medical emergencies, fire outbreaks, and attacks to reduce damage and help with crisis management.

The actor, who is known for his role as Major Pratap Chauhan in the movie 'Prahar,' lived with soldiers for more than two weeks during the **Kargil War, which was fought between India and Pakistan from May to July 1999 in Jammu and Kashmir. The war claimed the lives of around 527 Indian soldiers.**

Expressing his gratitude for the soldiers, Nana said, "Our greatest weapon is not the Bofors, nor the AK, but our jawans."

INDIAN COMPOUND WOMEN'S TEAM SECURES HAT TRICK OF GOLD MEDALS AT ARCHERY WORLD CUP

The Indian compound women's team clinched the gold medal at the Archery World Cup Stage 3 on **June 22, 2024**. The nation's top archers, Jyothi Surekha Vennam, Aditi Swami, and Parneet Kaur, emerged victorious against sixth-ranked Estonia in a tightly contested final, winning 232-229.

In archery, three kinds of bows are used: compound, barebow and recurve. Compound bows provide greater accuracy and power over a longer range and are simpler to draw, aim, and shoot.

+ VOCABULARY +

IAF - Indian Air Force - *It is the air arm of the Indian Armed Forces. Its primary mission is to secure Indian airspace and to conduct aerial warfare.*

SHORT STORY: NEVER TRUST AN UNFAMILIAR PERSON TOO QUICKLY

Long ago, in a temple, lived a sage who was well-respected in society. He had many disciples who visited him regularly and presented him with food, clothing, etc. However, the sage sold most of the presents that he felt were not useful to make money and kept all his cash in a pouch, which he consistently carried with him. He rarely trusted anyone with his cash pouch.

One day, a thief visited the temple to steal money and saw the sage. He found that the sage was carrying a pouch and never parted with it. He speculated that a large amount of cash might be in the pouch.

Hence, the thief came up with a plan for stealing that pouch. He decided to become the sage's most trusted pupil by persuading him with his kind words. After a few days, the thief went back to the temple. Falling at the sage's feet, he said, "I'm tired of this life, oh sage! I thus urge you to lead me down the right path and consider me your disciple." The sage agreed. The thief, thus, became the sage's constant companion and assisted the sage in all his daily tasks. Although the sage was delighted to have such a devoted follower, he never trusted the devotee with his pouch.

As the days went by, the thief grew frustrated. A few days later, the sage got an invitation to a housewarming ceremony and decided to take his new disciple with him. Before leaving, he carefully packed everything and slipped the cash pouch into his Kurta's pocket.

After walking for almost three hours, the sage and his disciple spotted a river. The tired sage decided to freshen up; he urged his fraud disciple to guard the bags while he went to have a cool dip in the river. The sage wrapped the pouch in a robe, fastened a rope to it and handed the whole thing to the thief without realising he was committing the biggest blunder of his life.

The fraudster finally got what he wanted and fled with the pouch soon after the sage left for a bath. The sage got back after some time, only to find both the bag and the thief missing. The sage was alarmed and looked all over but couldn't locate the trickster or the bag in question. The discontented sage was thus left with no choice but to return empty-handed the next morning.

Moral: "Don't trust everything you see; even salt looks like sugar."

JULY

EDIT

USE OF AI FOR SELF-PRESCRIPTION POSES RISK TO HUMAN LIFE, WARNS DOCTORS

On National Doctors' Day **(July 1)**, healthcare professionals voiced their concern over the growing trend of patients depending on internet search results for serious diseases. They claimed that the use of artificial intelligence (AI) for self-diagnosis and medication might endanger people's lives.

"Misusing or overusing medication can increase the risk of severe medical complications, causing harmful symptoms, including nausea, convulsions (fits) and even death," a health professional stated on **July 1, 2024.**

AI relies on data input, and in the medical field, data has to be accurate to guarantee a perfect diagnosis (identifying a disease) and provide the best treatment; however, common people cannot provide 100% accurate data.

"Dosages matter to ensure the best treatment for any ailment, and if that input is wrongly provided, the result could be disastrous, even leading to fatalities (death) in certain cases," a doctor warned.

"The Internet in general and AI in particular must be seen as a support function and not to trust blindly." Moreover, the "Internet, especially AI, is developed and dominated by the Western world, the US... Such information may or may not be suitable for people in India," argued another physician.

+ PROVERBS & PHRASES +

'No pain, no gain'

Meaning: *There is no success without hard work.*
Example: *"Study ten hours every day to crack the exam. I know it's tough, but remember, no pain, no gain," said the teacher.*

DID YOU KNOW THIS TERM?

"Commence"
pronounced as **"kuh-mens"**
Meaning (Verb): *To begin; start.*
Sentence: *The meeting is scheduled to commence at noon.*

BAJAJ AUTO LAUNCHES WORLD'S FIRST CNG-POWERED MOTORCYCLE 'FREEDOM 125'

Two-wheeler major Bajaj Auto's Freedom 125 is available in three variants starting at Rs 95,000 (ex-showroom).

The bike launched on **July 5, 2024,** is equipped with a 125-CC engine that can switch between CNG and petrol options. The capacity of the CNG tank is 2 kg, while that of the petrol tank is 2 litres. The CNG tank has a mileage of 102 km per kg and the petrol tank has a mileage of 65 km/l.

Vehicles powered by compressed natural gas (CNG) are superior to the petrol variants because they produce fewer greenhouse gases and pollutants, offer better mileage and are less prone to explosions. CNG is also cheaper than petrol.

SUDOKU

	1			2				8
	5	2			3		1	9
8	6	9	5	1			3	
6		3	7	5	8	9	2	1
		7	2			5	4	
2	9	5	6		1	3		
9	3	6	1	8			7	
4	2			7	6	8		
5	7	8	4	9		1	6	3

MATH PUZZLE

How many times in a day are the hands of a clock in a straight line but opposite in direction?

A) 20
B) 22
C) 24
D) 48

HOW TO BE CREATIVE ?

Name two occupations that you believe AI will not be able to replace and explain why you believe so.

ODISHA CM CONGRATULATED SAND ARTIST FOR WINNING GOLD IN INTERNATIONAL CHAMPIONSHIP

Odisha Chief Minister Mohan Charan Majhi congratulated sand artist Sudarsan Pattnaik for winning the Golden Sand Master Award on **July 12, 2024** at the International Sand Sculpture Championship held in St. Petersburg, Russia.

As many as 21 master sand sculptors from different corners of the world participated in this championship. The theme of the contest was history, mythology and fairy tales.

Pattnaik, the only participant from India, created a sand Ratha (chariot) of Lord Jagannath with his devotee Balaram Das, who is a 14th-century Odia poet.

In 2014, Sudarsan Pattnaik from Puri, Odisha, for his seashore sand arts, was honoured with the Padma Shri, India's fourth-highest civilian award.

<u>INSPIRATION</u>: ONE CHILD, ONE TEACHER, ONE PEN, AND ONE BOOK CAN CHANGE THE WORLD

In the beautiful Swat Valley of Pakistan, a young girl named Malala Yousafzai grew up with dreams of going to school and learning.

The Yousafzai family is known for backing female education. Ziauddin, Malala's father, was a teacher and ran a girl's school. He ensured Malala had equal access to a formal education alongside boys.

Life in Swat Valley was not peaceful. The region was under the influence of the Taliban, a terrorist organisation that believed girls should not attend school. However, Malala was adamant that she would not give up her studies.

On her way to school, she hid her school bag to avoid being tracked down by the Taliban.

At 11 years of age, she began writing letters for BBC Urdu as "a seventh-grade schoolgirl from Swat." She wrote about her life under the Taliban, the closing of girls' schools, and her strong desire to keep learning. Soon, her identity came to light, and the Taliban decided to kill her.

On October 9, 2012, something terrible happened.

Malala was on her way home from school on a bus when a Taliban gunman boarded the bus and shot her in the head.

Malala was then flown to the United Kingdom for urgent medical treatment, and miraculously, she survived. Instead of being silenced by fear, Malala became even more determined to fight for girls' education. While recovering in the UK, she co-authored the book "I Am Malala," which became a global bestseller. Her story of courage touched millions of hearts around the world. Malala's journey didn't stop there. She continued her education and graduated from Oxford University in 2020 in Philosophy, Politics, and Economics.

Today, she travels the world, speaking out for the rights of girls and inspiring others with her story.

She became the youngest person to win the Nobel Peace Prize in 2014 for her work "against the suppression of children and young people and for the right of all children to education."

Since 2013, Malala Day has been observed globally on her birthday, July 12, each year to recall how a little girl went on to teach the world, "With guns, you can kill terrorists; with education, you can kill terrorism."

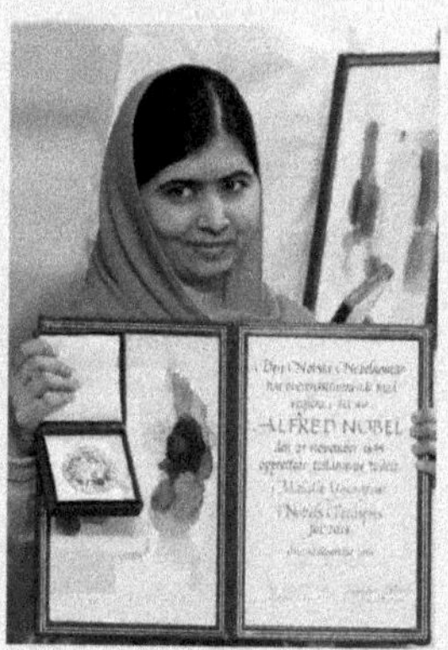

EXOTIC ANIMALS:
AXOLOTLS: A CREATURE THAT REGENERATES ITS ORGANS!

Imagine a creature that never outgrows its youthful charm and can regenerate its limbs. Welcome to the world of axolotls! These enchanting amphibians, often called 'Mexican walking fish,' are not fish but a type of salamander (a lizard-like amphibian).

Axolotls captivate scientists and pet enthusiasts with their unique ability to regrow limbs and organs throughout their lives, a condition known as 'neoteny.'

Axolotls thrive in the lakes and canals of Mexico City. They possess a distinct appearance, with feathery external gills, wide heads, and charming smiles. What sets them apart is their remarkable regenerative abilities.

Lose a limb? No problem! Axolotls can regrow not only limbs but also parts of their spinal cord, heart, and even their brain. Unfortunately, habitat loss and pollution have put these magnificent creatures at grave risk of extinction in the wild. However, they thrive in captivity, where their extraordinary abilities continue to fascinate and inspire.

ON THIS DAY OF JULY 31:

J.K. Rowling was born in 1965. She is the author of Harry Potter, a seven-volume fantasy series.

MANN KI BAAT: MATH OLYMPIAD WINNERS TALK ABOUT THE IMPORTANCE OF MATH

On July 28, PM Modi also addressed participants of the International Mathematics Olympiad, in which India was ranked fifth among 100 countries and won four golds and one silver.

Arjun Gupta, one of the participants from the International Mathematics Olympiad, shared what sparked his interest in the subject: "Maths helps us to develop problem-solving ability, which not only helps in one subject but also every aspect of life."

Aditya and Siddharth from Pune attributed their win to the opportunity and learning they got from their math teacher, Prakash.

Rushil Mathur said that math is not only about logical thinking but also about creativity because it helps students think out of the box while solving questions.

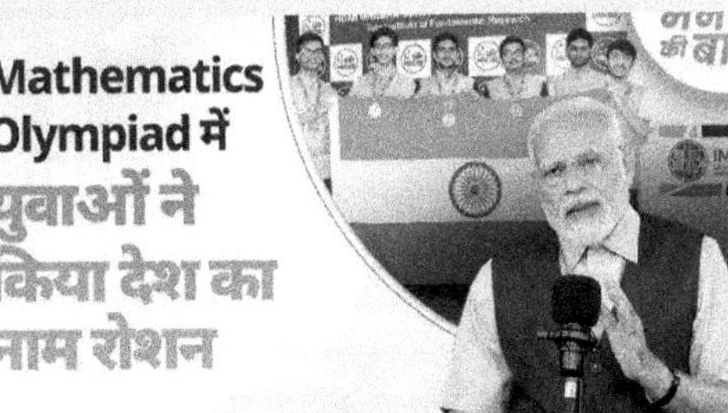

'IRON MAN' ROBERT DOWNEY JR. MAKES A COMEBACK TO MARVEL AS DOCTOR DOOM

On **July 28, 2024,** it was revealed that Hollywood star Robert Downey Jr. will be seen as the villain Doctor Victor von Doom in a new 'Avengers' movie titled 'Avengers: Doomsday,' which is due to be released in May 2026 and will be directed by the Russo brothers.

The 59-year-old actor and 2024 Oscar winner starred in "Iron Man," the Marvel movie universe's debut film, in 2008.

His last Marvel movie, 'Avengers: End Game', was released in 2019.

Marvel's highest-grossing film to date, 'Avengers: Endgame' (2019), earned \$2.8 billion worldwide. [1 billion = 100 crore; \$1 = Rs. 85.50 (as of Dec 31, 2024)]. Downey starred in 10 Marvel films, including the "Iron Man" series, "The Incredible Hulk," "The Avengers," "Captain America: Civil War," "Avengers: Infinity War," and "Avengers: Endgame."

+ DRAW WITH US +

+ PROVERBS AND PHRASES +

'Add insult to injury'

Meaning: *To make an unfair or unacceptable situation even worse.*

Example: *Neeraj's car broke down in the middle of nowhere, and then, to add insult to injury, it started to rain.*

PROFESSION: START EARNING BY GIVING DIETARY ADVICE TO ATHLETES!!!

Job title: *Sports Nutritionist*

Job description: *Nutrition is usually a major concern for athletes, particularly when trying to gain muscle mass or preparing for a particular event. Sports nutritionists are experts who advise athletes on a diet that helps improve their functional and physical capacities.*

Responsibilities:
• Keeping track of their patient's (mostly athlete's) progress or current objectives.
• Informing athletes about healthy eating habits.
• Preparing meal plans or recovery strategies for the sportsperson.
• Tracking the athletes' daily routines.
• Staying updated about the latest developments in the field of nutrition to provide the best counselling to the sportsperson under supervision.

Skills required: To pursue a Bachelor in Sports Science or B.Sc. (Food Science and Nutrition) in dietetics or nutrition, a student must pass the 12th standard board exam in science. Earning the Board Certified Specialist in Sports Dietetics (CCSD) certificate will give you an edge over others.

The best colleges that offer sports nutrition courses are:
In India: National Sports University-Manipur, Netaji Subhas National Institute of Sports - Patiala
Abroad:
Universidad Europea- Real Madrid ,University of Hull,-England

Salary: In India, the estimated yearly salary for a sports nutritionist is between Rs. 4 lakh and Rs. 6 lakh; the exact amount depends on years of experience. A sports nutritionist in the US makes between $65k and $80k a year.
$1 is traded for Rs. 85.50 (as updated on Dec 31, 2024).

INDIA HAS 26.52 CRORE STUDENTS IN SCHOOLS AND 4.33 CRORE IN HIGHER EDUCATION: ECONOMIC SURVEY

According to the Economic Survey 2023–24, presented by Finance Minister Nirmala Sitharaman on **July 22, 2024,**

India has "more than 11 crore learners in skilling institutions."

There has been a significant rise in enrolment in higher education driven by disadvantaged sections, along with a faster growth in female enrolment.

With the backdrop of developing concerns like artificial intelligence (AI), the nation has to create 78 lakh new non-agricultural jobs every year till 2030 to accommodate its growing workforce.

PARIS OLYMPICS 2024: 22-YEAR-OLD MANU BHAKER BECOMES FIRST INDIAN WOMAN SHOOTER TO WIN MEDAL

On **July 28, 2024,** Manu Bhaker secured a historic bronze medal in the women's 10 m pistol event with a score of 221.7 in the final, becoming the first Indian women's shooter to win a medal at the Olympics.

South Korea's Oh Ye Jin, with 243.2 points, won the gold.

"I read a lot of Gita and all, so what was going through my mind was its teachings……You know you focus on your karma and not on the outcome of the Karma', said the Olympic medal winner.

+ LINGUISTIC LEAPS: FLUENCE TO FINESSE +

I feel sad   -To-   I feel blue

'Cold feet'
Meaning: *Becoming nervous*

Example: *It was Shila's turn to address the crowd, and she was getting cold feet seeing the number of spectators.*

EAM JAISHANKAR UNVEILS MAHATMA GANDHI'S STATUE IN TOKYO

External Affairs Minister (EAM) S. Jaishankar began his Japan visit by inaugurating the statue of Mahatma Gandhi in Tokyo on **July 28, 2024**.

"Bapu's (Mahatma Gandhi's) achievements continue to inspire us to this day, and his message of peace and non-violence is timeless. His principles are even more relevant today when the world sees so much conflict, tension and polarisation," the EAM said at the event.

"Happy to learn….the heart of the Indian community in Tokyo would.. be soon named as the Gandhi Park," said Jaishankar.

Japan's Parliamentary Vice-Minister for Foreign Affairs, Masahiro Komura, said the statue of Mahatma Gandhi will become a familiar symbol of Japan-India friendship.

HEALTH: WHY TREKKING IS GOOD FOR US?

If you prefer mountains over beaches, chances are high that you love trekking too or want to try it at least once. But trekking is not just a thrilling activity; it offers a variety of physical and psychological benefits. Spending hours on the trail, climbing rocks, and ascending slopes keeps your entire body active, boosting strength, agility, and cardio fitness.

Enjoying an active holiday amid nature helps remove tension and anxieties. Hiking can improve cardiovascular strength since the heart has to work harder to meet the oxygen requirement.

This boosts the flow of blood to the muscles and brain, hence enhancing both the cardiovascular and respiratory systems' efficiency.

+ FACTS +

THE NILE IS ACKNOWLEDGED AS THE WORLD'S LONGEST RIVER, SPANNING AN INCREDIBLE 6,695 KILOMETRES!

Note: Located in northeastern Africa, the Nile flows into the Mediterranean Sea. Though it passes through eleven countries—Tanzania, Uganda, the Democratic Republic of the Congo, Rwanda, Burundi, Ethiopia, Kenya, Eritrea, South Sudan, Sudan, and Egypt—the Nile is most frequently associated with Egypt. The Nile River has two primary tributaries, the White Nile and the Blue Nile.

The White Nile is the longest, extending approximately 3,700 kilometres from Lake Victoria in East Africa. The Blue Nile, on the other hand, originates in Ethiopia and accounts for 80% of the Nile's water. The Nile supports a rich range of wildlife, including crocodiles, hippos, and a variety of fish species such as Nile perch and catfish. The river also acts as a major migration path for birds like storks and herons.

+ PROVERBS AND PHRASES +

'Live and learn'

Meaning: *To gain knowledge and wisdom through experiences, including mistakes and failures.*

Example: *"I thought I could trust him, but he betrayed me. Anyway, that is how we live and learn."*

AUGUST

EDIT

WHY ARE SCIENTISTS PLANNING TO PLACE SAMPLES OF ENDANGERED CREATURES ON THE MOON?

Specimens need to be preserved at significantly lower temperatures (-320 degrees Fahrenheit or -196 degrees Celsius). This requires a constant supply of liquid nitrogen, electricity and human labour, and any interruptions might completely wipe out a collection.

A specimen is a tiny sample or piece of an animal or plant that scientists keep to study and learn more about it.

To guarantee the long-term preservation of endangered animal samples, scientists on **August 2, 2024,** suggested installing a lunar storage centre that would function similarly to a refrigerator situated near the poles, in permanently shadowed regions with temperatures below -196°C. **This would shield them from the impacts of wars, natural calamities, and climate change without requiring constant electricity or human intervention.**

+ GENERAL KNOWLEDGE +

In which continent is the "Snake Island" located?
1. *Asia*
2. *Africa*
3. *North America*
4. *South America*

The famous "Snake Island" is located in South America's Brazil.

Note: Ilha da Queimada Grande, also called "Snake Island," is an island off the coast of Brazil. It is located in the Atlantic Ocean, around 144 km from São Paulo. Around 2,000 to 4,000 golden lancehead vipers, one of the deadliest snakes in the world, can be found on the island. These snakes are responsible for 90% of snakebite deaths in Brazil. The strong and fast-acting poison of golden lanceheads can melt the muscles around the bite sites and kill a human in less than an hour. Lanceheads can reach lengths of over half a metre. For the safety of humans and snakes, Queimada Grande is only accessible to the Brazilian Navy and a small group of biodiversity conservation researchers.

INSPIRATION:
PLASTIC MAN OF INDIA: THE MAN WHO TURNED 'TRASH' INTO 'TREASURE'

Recycled plastic debris (waste) has gained popularity as an environmentally acceptable and sustainable substitute for conventional materials used in the construction of roads. The idea of using waste plastic in road construction was first proposed by Indian scientist Dr. Rajagopalan Vasudevan.

Dr. Rajagopalan Vasudevan: India's "plastic man"

The 73-year-old Dr. Vasudevan is a professor in Madurai, Tamil Nadu. He specialises in waste management research. Plastic releases harmful chemicals that pose a threat to living beings and what's startling is that it takes 400 years to break down. For this reason, the government passed regulations to ban single-use plastic.

Dr. Vasudevan devised a method to recycle plastic waste, that can be used to construct streets that are durable and cheap.

During his visit to Thiagarajar College, the late Dr. APJ Abdul Kalam, a scientist and former president of India, urged Dr. Vasudevan to construct the college's first plastic-paved road."He asked me to make the roads grey because black roads absorb and trap heat," shared Dr. Vasudevan.

In 2002, Dr. Vasudevan used bitumen mixed with plastic to pave a 60-foot road inside the campus. Even today, the road remains undamaged. In 2006, Dr. Vasudevan received a patent for his technique. In 2018, he was awarded Padma Shri, India's fourth highest civilian honour for his crucial research.

How are roads constructed from plastic?

Although it is difficult to construct roadways out of plastic, the process is fascinating. First, the plastic is shredded into tiny pieces, dust particles are eliminated and then all the crushed bits are combined with hot gravel. The mixture is then heated to 160°C and is poured on the hot asphalt road.

How safe are the plastic roads?

When the Central Pollution Control Board reviewed the efficacy of plastic roads, it found that the streets exhibited no regular defects even after four years. Plastic-constructed highways are found to be sustainable, cost-effective and reliable. Bitumen-plastic roads enhance the roadways' weight-bearing capacity and longevity.

They also showed greater strength against rain-induced damage. Chennai was one of the first cities globally to adopt this technology.

In 2004, the municipality ordered the construction of 1,000 km of plastic roads. By July 2021, nearly 703 km of national highways and approximately 40,000 kilometres of rural roads had been built using this method.

ON THIS DAY OF AUGUST 12:

In 1919, Vikram Sarabhai was born. He is known as the "Father of Indian space program," and pioneered space research in India.

INSPIRATION: DOKKA SEETHAMMA

Dokka Seethamma, fondly remembered as 'Apara Annapurna' (Goddess of Food), was a remarkable woman whose life was dedicated to feeding the poor and hungry.

Every day, Seethamma would cook large quantities of food and serve it to anyone who came to her door hungry. Her selfless service soon earned her the love and respect of her community.

What makes Seethamma's story even more extraordinary is the sheer scale of her efforts. It is said that she would feed hundreds of people daily, never turning anyone away. Her kitchen was always bustling, filled with the aroma of freshly cooked meals. She managed this incredible feat with the help of her family and the donations she received from the villagers, who admired her noble mission. Seethamma's dedication went beyond just feeding the hungry. She was known for her kindness and empathy.

She would often listen to the troubles of those who came to her for food, offering them not just a meal but also emotional support. Her home became a place of support where people felt valued and cared for.

Seethamma's work did not go unnoticed. Her reputation spread far and wide, and she was revered as a living saint. People would travel from distant places to seek her blessings and witness her generosity firsthand. Even as she grew older, her commitment to feeding the hungry never wavered. She continued her noble mission until her last breath in 1909.

JAMES CAMERON'S 'AVATAR 3' OFFICIALLY TITLED 'FIRE AND ASH'

Director James Cameron and stars Zoe Saldana and Sam Worthington revealed the first official title for Avatar's next franchise, 'Avatar: Fire and Ash,' during the Disney Fan Event D23 expo, held on **August 10, 2024.**

"It's an insane adventure and a feast for the eyes," Cameron said about the upcoming Avatar movie, which is expected to be released on 19 December 2025 in the USA.

Cameron shot 'Fire and Ash' back-to-back with 2022's 'Avatar: The Way of Water,' which portrays the war between humanity and the Na'vi after the greedy Resources Development Administration returns to the alien moon of Pandora. 'Fire and Ash' will pick up soon after those events.

Cameron's first Avatar movie, released in 2009, is the highest-grossing movie of all time at $2.9 billion. [1 billion = 100 crores; $1 = Rs. 85.50 (as of December 31, 2024)].

SUDOKU

7	3	8					9	
			6	2				
	4					5	1	
2	1	5	4	8			6	9
	8		2	7	5	4		
3			9	6	1			
	6	3	8	5	7	9	2	4
		7	1				5	3
8		9		4	2	1	7	6

MATH PUZZLE

Add me to myself and multiply by 4. Divide me by 8 and you will have me once more.

What number am I?

WORLD ORGAN DONATION DAY: "SAVE A LIFE AFTERLIFE"

Every year on August 13, World Organ Donation Day is observed to dismiss myths around organ donation and highlight the importance of organ donation.

What is organ donation?
The process of surgically removing an organ from a donor —a living or dead individual— and implanting the removed organ into someone who needs it is known as organ donation. The receiver is someone who is terminally ill with organ failure and will not be able to live without an organ transplant. Organs that can be donated include the liver, kidney, pancreas, lung, heart, intestine, cornea, bone, tissues, etc.

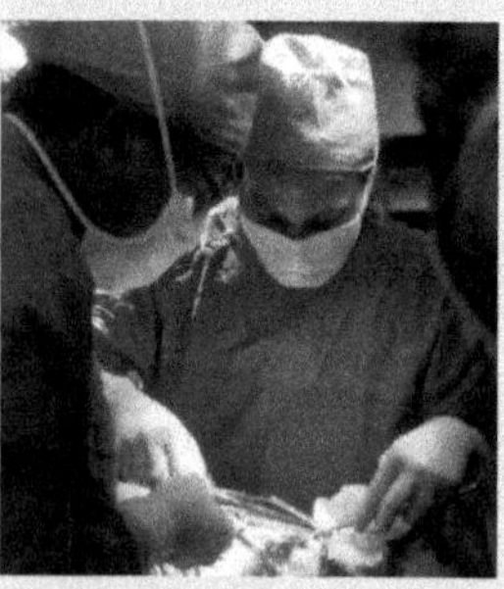

Two categories of organ donation are:

1. Living organ donation: This refers to the process of removing an organ from a living, healthy individual and transplanting it into a person who has terminal organ failure. This is generally done in the event of liver (upto 60% of liver can be donated as the liver can grow back to its usual size) or kidney failure (donor can live on one kidney).

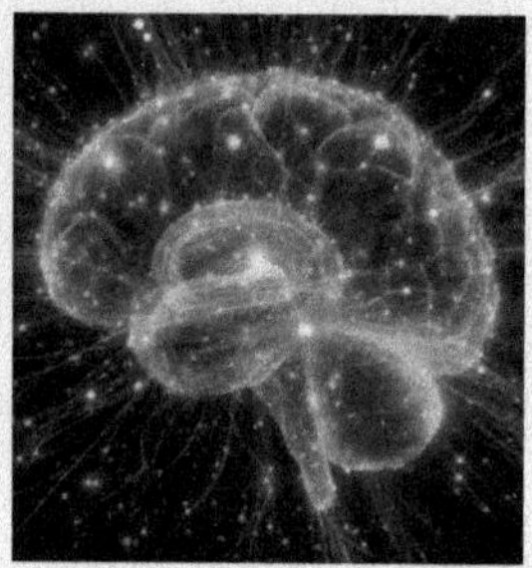

2. Donation of Deceased Organs: In India, organ donation is allowed mostly in cases involving brain death. Donations made after a cardiac death are prevalent, but mostly in Western nations.
The permanent loss of all brain functions, including brainstem functions, is known as brain death.

India has the lowest organ donation rate in the world, with only 0.1% of the population donating their organs after death, compared to 70–80% in Western countries, experts noted on National Organ Donation Day (August 3).
"One deceased person can save up to eight lives, so you can understand how important organ donation is," said senior expert on Transplantation.

According to 2022 data, Telangana had the highest number of organ donors after death (194), followed by Tamil Nadu (156) and Karnataka (151).
"We have to harvest the organs in 12 hours, and the transplant has to happen within a short window," said an expert.

World Organ Donation Day: Background The first individual to donate an organ was Ronald Lee Herrick. He gave his kidney to his twin brother in 1954, and the physician who performed this successful organ transplant procedure was Dr. Joseph Murray. Dr. Murray received the Nobel Prize in Physiology and Medicine in 1990 in recognition of his contributions to the organ transplantation domain.

+ *DRAW WITH US* +

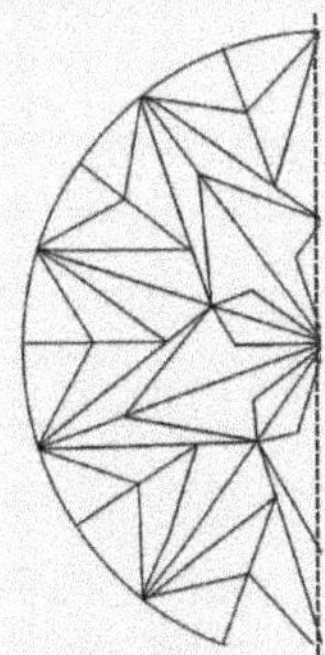

CENTRE LAUNCHES KRISHI DSS, PROVIDING FARMERS WITH REAL-TIME DATA ON WEATHER, SOIL, AND CROP HEALTH

The Centre on **August 16, 2024,** unveiled the Krishi-Decision Support System (DSS), a digital geospatial platform, to give the country's farmers access to real-time data on weather information, soil conditions, crop health and water levels in reservoirs.

Farmers Welfare Bhagirath Choudhary.

"This information helps in understanding crop rotation practices and promotes sustainable agriculture by encouraging the cultivation of diverse crops," he added.

The platform offers satellite images, groundwater levels and soil health information that is easily accessible from anywhere at any time, said Union Minister of State for Agriculture and

It includes individual advisories to farmers and early disaster warnings in cases of pest attacks, heavy rain, hail storms, etc.

Drought monitoring will help farmers stay ahead of droughts by providing near-real-time information on various indicators such as soil moisture, water storage, crop conditions, and dry spells. Additionally, crop weather monitoring will keep farmers informed about how the weather is impacting crops, harvest status, and crop residue burning.

The 'one-nation-one-soil' information system provides comprehensive data about soil type, soil pH, soil health, etc. This data will help determine crop suitability and land capability for implementing soil and water conservation measures.

Panel discussions were held to explore the possible uses of space technology in agriculture.

+ LINGUISTIC LEAPS: FLUENCE TO FINESSE +

"This is an expensive car   -To-   This is a lavish car"

SIGNIFICANCE OF 'NATIONAL SCIENCE DAY'

On August 23, 2023, the Indian Space Research Organisation (ISRO) achieved a significant milestone when the Chandrayaan-3 lander and rover touched down on the lunar surface.

In recognition of this success, Prime Minister Narendra Modi proclaimed August 23 to be observed as "National Space Day" in India.

With this feat, India became the first country to land a spacecraft close to the lunar south pole and the fourth in the world to land a spacecraft on the lunar surface.

What is Chandrayaan-3?

Chandrayaan-3, India's third lunar mission and its second attempt to soft-land on the moon, was launched on July 14, 2023, from the Satish Dhawan Space Centre in Sriharikota, Andhra Pradesh.

The spacecraft entered lunar orbit on August 5, 2023. On August 23, 2023, the lander successfully landed close to the lunar south pole.

Principal conclusions:

• *Moon's shocking surface temperature:* Experts expected the lunar temperature to be between 20 and 30 degrees Celsius, but they were taken aback by Chandra's Surface Thermophysical Experiment (ChaSTE), which recorded temperatures as high as 70 degrees Celsius.

• *Validation of lunar surface elements*: Near the Moon's South Pole, the 'Pragyan' rover verified the presence of sulphur.

Additionally, traces of elements like silicon, oxygen, aluminium, calcium, iron, chromium, titanium, and manganese were also found.

Objectives of National Space Day:

In addition to celebrating the accomplishments of the Chandrayaan-3 mission, National Space Day aims to encourage the next generation of space enthusiasts, technicians, and scientists to pursue space research.

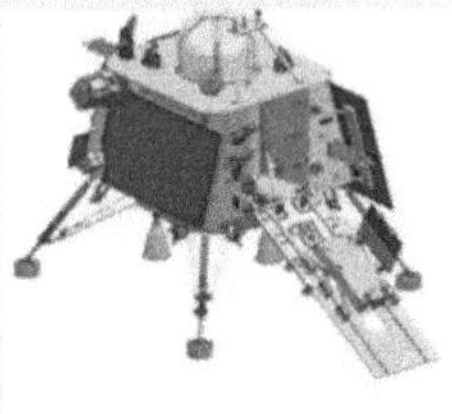

Rover on Ramp   Rover Deployed from Lander

3,000-YEAR-OLD TREE KNOCKED OVER BY POWERFUL TYPHOON IN JAPAN

A 26-meter-high cedar tree (a type of evergreen coniferous tree) on Yakushima Island in the Kagoshima region of southwestern Japan was uprooted by Typhoon Shanshan.

With winds reaching 168.48 kilometres per hour, Typhoon Shanshan wreaked devastation on the island from **August 27 to August 29, 2024,** causing seven fatalities, over 120 injuries and damage to over 1,000 residences.

Yakushima Island, known for its more than 1,000-year-old "Yakusugi" cedars, was designated as a World Natural Heritage site in 1993. These cedar trees grow between 500 meters and 1600 meters above sea level and have a minimum lifespan of 500 years; the reason behind their longevity is their capability to withstand harsh climates.

SECOND RECEIVER OF NEURALINK BRAIN CHIP SHOWING STEADY PROGRESS

The brain-computer interface company Neuralink has confirmed early progress with its second participant. Alex, who received his Neuralink implant in July 2024, "The surgery went well—Alex was discharged the following day, and his recovery has been smooth," Neuralink updated.

The coin-sized Neuralink chip is implanted beneath the skull through robotic surgery. Once inserted, the chip helps read brain signals and links to a computer or smartphone.

With the chip, the patient has been improving his ability to play video games and has begun

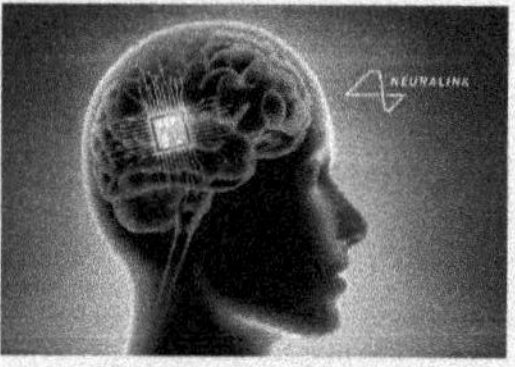

learning how to use computer-aided design (CAD) software to design 3D objects.

The world's richest man, Elon Musk said on **August 22, 2024,** that if all goes well,

there will be hundreds of people with Neuralink brain chips within a few years. The chip can help restore full body control in paralysed people.

According to Neuralink, this operation marks an important phase in developing a powerful link that will improve quadriplegic individuals' ability to use digital devices and restore movement to some extent.

Quadriplegia is a condition caused by a severe spinal cord injury in which all four limbs are paralysed.

"Additionally, we plan to enable the Link to interact with the physical world, allowing users to feed themselves and move more independently by controlling a robotic arm or their wheelchair," the Musk-run company noted.

+ GENERAL KNOWLEDGE +

Who founded Nalanda University?

A. *Samudragupta*
B. *Chandragupta*
C. *Kumaragupta*
D. *Harsh Vardhana*

Nalanda is the world's first residential university.

Note: In the fifth century BC, Kumaragupta of the Gupta dynasty constructed Nalanda University. Historians claim that this centre of education, excellence, and cultural interaction flourished between the 5th century CE to 1200 CE and was considered an important learning centre. Muhammad Bakhtiyar Khilji set fire to the library at Nalanda University and destroyed this esteemed centre of learning. On January 9, 2009, Nalanda University was added to the UNESCO World Heritage List. Dr. A.P.J. Abdul Kalam, the former president of India, suggested reviving historic Nalanda. In 2010, Nalanda University was re-established and is now recognised as a prominent national institution. It is situated in Rajgir, in Bihar's Nalanda district.

Triumph Daytona launched at Rs 9.72 lakh in India

Triumph Motorcycles Ltd., a UK-owned motorcycle manufacturer, unveiled the Daytona 660 in three different colour choices on **August 29, 2024.**

The Daytona 660 features dual-channel ABS, a transparent windscreen, three riding modes (rain, road, and sport), and a split LED headlamp. The Daytona 660, the most powerful model in the 660 series, has a 660cc inline three-cylinder engine, which generates 95 horsepower. It comes with a 14-litre fuel tank that fuels a lengthy ride and features Showa USD forks at the front and a Showa mono-shock at the rear for a customisable ride. **Anti-lock Braking System (ABS) prevents a motorcycle's wheels from locking up when the brakes are applied suddenly, thus preventing skidding.**

SEPTEMBER

EDIT

NAMIBIA PLANS TO KILL 723 ANIMALS TO FEED ITS DROUGHT-AFFECTED POPULATION

On **September 1, 2024**, Namibia disclosed its plan to slaughter hundreds of its most majestic wild animals to feed its 14 lakh residents, who are battling a hunger crisis.

There are 723 animals on the kill list, including 83 elephants, 30 hippopotamuses, 60 buffalo, 50 impalas, 100 blue wildebeests, 300 zebras, and 100 elands, a type of antelope.

Over 150 animals have been slaughtered until now; the government has hired professionals for this purpose to avoid human casualties. This mass slaughtering will also help reduce human-animal conflicts over food and water.

Namibia is located in drought-prone southern Africa and declared a national emergency due to severe droughts in 2013, 2016, and 2019.

+ PROVERBS & PHRASES +

'At the drop of a hat'

Meaning: *To do something immediately, without delay.*

Example: *"All the arrangements have been made; we can leave at the drop of a hat," said Ravi.*

IMAGE DECODER

STUDENTS MUST USE KNOWLEDGE TO HELP UNDERPRIVILEGED SECTIONS: PRESIDENT MURMU

"Based on knowledge, they (students) should create software, healthcare products and marketing strategies that help in the development of everyone, especially the underprivileged sections and also promote sustainability," President Murmu said while addressing a university on **September 3, 2024.**

The president also advised students to try to achieve excellence in every task, adding that they must have heard the saying 'Chase excellence and success will follow'.

"Many times, it happens that some people consider having more money, a big house, a car, and other things as a sign of success. Students must understand the true meaning of success and work, which also improves the standard of living of others," the President said.

SUDOKU

	5					3	7	
8	3	1	4	2	7			5
9	7	4		8	6	1	2	3
3	8	6	1	4		2	5	7
7		5						
	4	9	7		2	8	3	6
5				7	4		9	8
	9		3		1			2
2				9			3	1

MATH PUZZLE

1. The day before yesterday, I was 25. Next year, I will be 28. This is true only one day a year. What day is my birthday?

2. How do I get 100 by using four sevens (7's) and one (1)?

FRESH FRUIT JUICE AND PACKAGED JUICES HARMFUL, EVEN THOUGH LABELLED AS 'HEALTHY', WARN EXPERTS

Packaged juices usually contain minimal fruit pulp and are unhealthy due to their high sugar content, posing the risk of diabetes and obesity, a rising health concern in the country. Consuming packaged fruit juices can also lead to weight gain, and other health issues.

"Packaged juices are not healthy at all. They are high in sugars and low in nutritional value. When it comes to nutrition, the percentage of fruit pulp is low, while artificial flavours, stabilisers and sugar/sweeteners/fructose syrup are generally very high," said a doctor from Fortis Hospital on **September 3, 2024.**

Doctors recommended having fresh fruits instead of juices (both fresh or packaged). It is because "when juice is prepared, the pulp is removed, along with its vitamins, minerals, and fibres also are removed," the expert said. Eating fresh fruits provides a balanced mix of vitamins, minerals, and antioxidants.

PARIS PARALYMPICS 2024: HISTORIC! INDIA CONCLUDED WITH 29 MEDALS, INCLUDING 7 GOLD

India's 21-year-old para-athlete Praveen Kumar won the gold medal in the Men's High Jump T64 with a jump of 2.08 meters on **September 6, 2024**. Noida's Praveen, who was born with a short leg, struggled with insecurity as a youngster but went on to win a silver medal at the Tokyo 2020 Paralympics, becoming the youngest para-athlete to do so; he was 18 at that time.

Nagaland's Hokato Hotozhe Sema secured the bronze for India in the men's shot put F57 final on **September 6, 2024,** with an impressive throw of 14.65 meters, marking his personal best. **"As an army man, I felt if Neeraj Chopra could do it for the Indian Army and India as an able-bodied athlete, as a para-athlete from the Indian army, why can't I?"** said Sema, an ex-soldier who was injured in a mine explosion in Jammu and Kashmir and lost his left leg below the knee.

Visually impaired Simran Sharma won India's first-ever medal (bronze) in the Women's 200m T12 category with a personal best time of 24.75 seconds. The 24-year-old was a gold medallist in the World Para Athletics Championship in Kobe, Japan, earlier in 2024.

With a spectacular closing ceremony held at the Stade de France on **September 8, 2024,** the Paralympic Games ended.

China finished first in the Paralympic medal standings with 94 gold, 76 silver, and 50 bronze. Great Britain took the second spot with 49 gold, 44 silver, and 31 bronze, and the United States of America came in third with 36 gold, 42 silver, and 27 bronze. India sent its biggest contingent, consisting of 84 athletes competing in 12 different sports and ended with the 18th spot on the medal tally after securing 7 gold, 9 silver, and 13 bronze medals, making it the most rewarding campaign for the country.

The International Paralympic Committee lists ten eligible disability types, including intellectual disabilities and physical disabilities such as limb deficiency, muscle power issues, and vision problems and those categories are denoted by codes such as F20, SH1 etc.

UP's Atal Residential School's girl student selected for ISRO visit

Shweta Satte, a class 7 student from Atal Residential School in Karsada, Varanasi, Uttar Pradesh, emerged as the school's topper on **September 8, 2024,** and will soon visit the Indian Space Research Organisation (ISRO).

She has been selected for an exclusive tour of ISRO, where she will have the opportunity to meet scientists and explore the mysteries of the universe.

This opportunity is part of the 'Utkrisht Atal program' that offers students practical experience with modern technologies and provides insights into India's space achievements. The workshop was held to guide students in various competitions, including Space Art and Best Product Development and Shweta emerged as the topper. Varanasi's Atal Residential School is offering free education to children who lost their families during the COVID-19 pandemic.

ON THIS DAY OF SEPTEMBER 23RD :

In 1846, astronomer Johann Gottfried Galle became the first person ever to observe the planet Neptune.

INDIA TO GET EYE DROP THAT CAN ELIMINATE THE USE OF READING GLASSES

PresVu Eye Drops can eliminate the use of reading glasses for presbyopia, a condition that occurs naturally with ageing, leading to difficulty focusing on close objects, particularly while reading a newspaper or book when held at arm's length.

It typically starts in the mid-40s and worsens until about the late 60s. As per a report published on **September 9, 2024,** this prescription-based eye drop will help reduce dependency on reading glasses and can improve daily life and productivity. Priced at Rs. 350, it was expected to be available from the first week of October 2024.

This lubricating eye drop is safe to use and doctors claim that it starts showing promising results within 15 minutes of application and can be used for years. Presbyopia is estimated to impact more than 10,800 crore individuals worldwide.

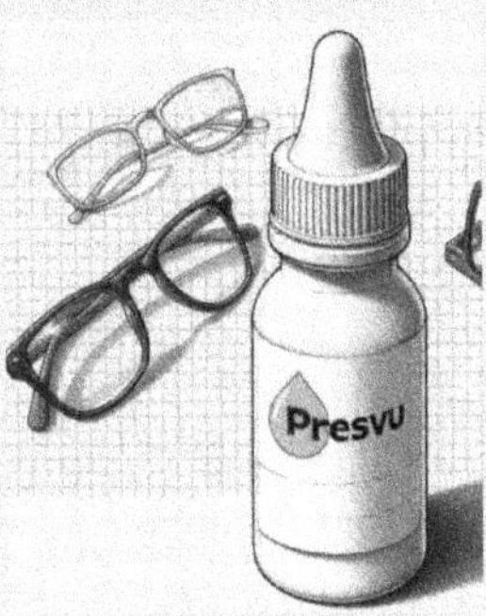

+ DRAW WITH US +

EXOTIC ANIMALS: STARTLING FACTS ABOUT THE UNDERSEA GIANT- JAPANESE SPIDER CRAB

Have you heard about the humongous Japanese spider crab that crawls on the ocean floor like a spider and can grow to gigantic proportions? This crab is known by the Japanese name 'taka-ashigani,' which translates to "tall legs crab."

Here are some incredible details on the species that are found off the southern coastlines of Honshū, Japan.

Eerie look!

The Japanese spider crab appears ridiculously large; it could literally tower over a human child with a leg span of 13 feet (4 metres)! Japanese spider crabs are the largest crabs known to exist and can weigh around forty pounds (16–20 kg) on average.

The marine monster has ten legs:

These crabs have eight walking legs and two clawed (cheliped) legs. Their legs often get severed by a predator or trawl net, but grow back eventually. If you still believe that these crabs aren't all that scary, then let us share that they have reportedly used their claws to chop off human fingers.

The scavengers:

These crabs do not swim; instead, they spend most of their time strolling on the seafloor trying to find food. These scavengers search the seafloor for deceased and rotting creatures rather than hunting themselves. They mostly consume algae, insects, and dead or decomposing fish.

They often have a 100-year lifespan!

The typical crab that you find in retail has a long lifespan. Hermit crabs can live well over 60 years, red crabs about 30 years, and blue crabs up to 8 years!

The Japanese spider crab, however, outweighs them all. It can live for at least a century, if not more and what is most horrifying about them all is that they become larger as they age. These crabs moult, losing their shells and gaining new ones that are a little bigger each time.

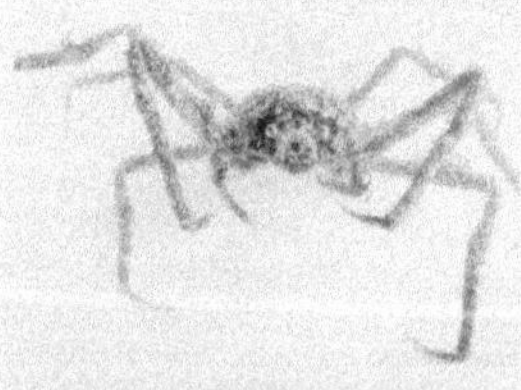

Possess excellent camouflage skills:

The Japanese spider crabs can easily blend in with the stony ocean floor to escape from the grasp of their predators. The young spider crabs adorn their

shells with kelp or sponges to enhance their ability to evade predators. However, fully mature Japanese spider crabs rely more on their sharp claws to fend off predators.

Conclusion:

Rising seawater temperatures have caused an alarming decrease in the Japanese spider crab population. Japan has tightened its laws prohibiting the fishing of Japanese spider crabs during specific times of the year to protect these amazing and enthralling underwater treasures from going extinct.

AUSTRALIAN ARMY TESTS DRIVERLESS ROBOTS FOR DANGEROUS MISSIONS

On **September 11, 2024,** the Australian Army began trials of an uncrewed robot, which can replace soldiers in risky areas and do the required observation in the future.

The robot, nicknamed GUS (Ground Uncrewed System), is equipped with cameras and sensors capable of providing surveillance for more than 30 days using battery power. An onboard liquid fuel generator recharges the battery when it is low to extend GUS's mission endurance even further. "GUS can detect moving objects and can then transmit this information to a remote operator," the ministry detailed.

GUS was initially developed, hoping it could protect rangers in Africa's vast national parks from armed invaders. However, the Australian Army chose to shift the robot from wildlife conservation to military purposes.

+ MATH PUZZLE +

I am an odd number. Take away one letter and I become even. What number am I?

HIGH SCREEN TIME IN PARENTS AND CHILDREN LINKED TO POORER LANGUAGE SKILLS; FACE-TO-FACE INTERACTION HELPS IMPROVE

Parents who use screens a lot also have children who use screens a lot and higher screen time is associated with poorer language skills, like weaker vocabulary, claimed scientists of Estonia on **September 12, 2024,** after analysing 421 children and their parents.

Analysing the language development of these children, the team found that children who used screens less scored higher in both grammar and vocabulary. No form of screen use had a positive effect on children's language skills.

It was noted that reading ebooks and playing educational games may offer language learning opportunities, especially for older children.

"The research shows that the most influential factor is everyday face-to-face parent-child verbal interaction," said the study's lead author.

77TH SENIOR NATIONAL AQUATIC CHAMPIONSHIPS 2024: KARNATAKA RETAINS TITLE

Karnataka bagged 17 gold medals, 12 silver medals and four bronze medals to clinch the top spot in the 77th Senior National Aquatic Championships 2024, held in Mangaluru from **September 10 to 13, 2024.** Maharashtra became the runner-up with 6 gold, 4 silver, and 4 bronze.
Karnataka also created a new record in the men's 4x100m freestyle. The 77th Senior National Aquatic Championships saw participants (men and women) competing in various swimming categories like 400m Individual Medley, 200m Backstroke, 100m Butterfly and Breaststroke.

The most popular and fastest swimming stroke is the front crawl, also known as freestyle.

INDIA DEFEATS CHINA IN A NAIL-BITING FINAL TO LIFT ASIAN HOCKEY CHAMPIONS TROPHY

The Indian men's hockey team kept the Tricolour flying high as it scored a 1-0 victory over China in the final of the Asian Champions Trophy at the scenic Moqi Hockey Training Base, China Daur Ethnic Park, Hulunbuir, on **September 17, 2024.**

In the first three quarters, the Harmanpreet-led team couldn't penetrate through the Chinese defence, but Jugraj Singh's goal in the 51st minute helped India seal its victory. Pakistan took third place in the six-team tournament after defeating Korea 5-2.

With this, India won the Men's Asian Champions Trophy for the fifth time and extended their record as the most successful nation in the competition that was launched in 2011.

FINANCE MINISTER SITHARAMAN LAUNCHED NEW PENSION SCHEME 'VATSALYA' FOR STUDENTS

Finance Minister Nirmala Sitharaman introduced NPS "Vatsalya," a new pension plan for minors (up to the age of 18 years) on **September 18, 2024.**

This pension scheme is a financial plan in which parents deposit money in their child's name for several years, which the child can later withdraw after retirement as a financial safeguard.

NPS 'Vatsalya' offers flexible investment options, allowing parents to make a minimum investment of Rs 1,000 per year in the name of the child, thus making it accessible to families from all economic backgrounds.

The NPS (New Pension Scheme) Vatsalya account can be opened online (eNPS) and offline in a nationalised bank, post office and PFRDA-accredited PoS. The guardian must submit identity and address proof along with the date of birth proof of the minor to open an NPS "Vatsalya" account.

NEURALINK'S BLINDSIGHT TO RESTORE VISION TO PEOPLE WHO LOST BOTH EYES

In yet another revolutionary invention, brain-computer interface company Neuralink has developed a Blindsight implant that can help vision restoration for individuals with severe visual impairments.

The Blindsight device from Neuralink will enable even those who have lost both eyes and their optic nerve to see. Provided the visual cortex is intact, it will even enable those who have been blind from birth to see for the first time.

"To set expectations correctly, the vision will at first be low resolution, but eventually, it has the potential to be better than natural vision and enable you to see in infrared, ultraviolet or even radar wavelengths," the world's richest man and owner of Neuralink, Elon Musk, explained on **September 18, 2024.**

The visual cortex is a critical part of the brain responsible for processing visual information. It is located in the occipital lobe, at the back of the brain, and plays a key role in interpreting the signals received from the eyes.

"Neuralink's Blindsight device represents a significant leap forward in assistive visual technologies. We look forward to seeing how this innovation can improve the lives of individuals with visual impairments," said a spokesperson for the FDA. The pioneering device has not yet begun human trials.

Elon Musk founded Neuralink in 2016 along with a team of seven scientists and engineers who were experts in areas such as neuroscience, biochemistry, and robotics.

The company had earlier developed a brain chip that can help restore full body control in people suffering from paralysis.

GUINEA BANS SINGLE-USE PLASTIC TO PROMOTE ENVIRONMENTAL PROTECTION

Guinea on **September 23, 2024**, banned the production, importation, distribution, and use of single-use plastic items and packaging.

Single-use plastic goods include straws, bags made of plastic, earbuds, bottles, and wrappers.

The goal of this initiative is to tackle pollution and other environmental hazards as well as to promote biodegradable packaging and public health.

The decree prohibits the disposal of plastic packaging in streets, public areas, bodies of water, or natural environments, both in urban and rural areas. Violators could face penalties such as business closure, product seizure, and fines.

Guinea (gi-nee) is a West African nation, bordered by the Atlantic Ocean on the west. Conakry is its capital.

HOW TO BE CREATIVE ?

Explain how reading books for an hour daily will foster self-development.

ON THIS DAY OF SEPTEMBER 18 :

In 1819, the French physicist Jean-Bernard-Léon Foucault was born. His "Foucault pendulum" provided experimental proof that Earth rotates on its axis.

CHIRANJEEVI ENTERS GUINNESS WORLD RECORDS AS MOST CREATIVE FILM STAR

Tollywood superstar K. Chiranjeevi, often referred to as Megastar in film circles, received the certificate from a Guinness World Records representative at an event in Hyderabad on **September 22, 2024.**
"I never expected to get Guinness World Records. Dance has been part of my life all these years of my film career," the actor said.

Chiranjeevi holds the record for the most "Industry Hits" in Telugu cinema. In his career spanning 45 years, the actor has performed 24,000 dance moves in 537 songs in his 156 films.

The 69-year-old Telugu actor has received numerous honours, including the Padma Bhushan (2006) and the Padma Vibhushan (2024) for his contribution to Indian cinema.

MUMBAI SCHOOLGIRL BECOMES WORLD'S YOUNGEST TO GET SHOULDER-LEVEL ARM TRANSPLANT

Anamta Aqeel Ahmad (15) from Mumbai has become the youngest person in history to receive an arm transplant from the shoulder level on **September 29, 2024.** The donor arm was collected from a 9-year-old girl who lived in Surat and was declared "brain dead."

Anamta was 13 when she accidentally touched a live electric wire, resulting in a massive shock with significant burns. Her right hand developed gangrene (infection) and had to be removed.

However, Anamta did not lose hope. "She even learnt afresh to write with her left hand and went to score 92 percent in her SSC examinations, including a staggering score of 98 marks in Hindi in school last year," said Anamta's father.

Anamta's family met Dr. Nilesh G. Satbhai at the Gleneagles Hospital in Mumbai, which specialises in such surgeries.

The surgery went on for nearly 12 hours, "The patient has recovered well and is in ICU for observation and shall be discharged in a fortnight," said Dr. Satbhai.

Dr. Satbhai explained that hand transplantation is a very complex procedure since the original injury often results in severe damage to the skin, blood vessels and nerves. He added the major challenge was to restore the blood circulation in the donor's hand within six hours to ensure it survives and functions well without any health risks to the beneficiary (Anamta); hence, the donated organ was airlifted to Mumbai.

HOW TO BE CREATIVE ?

Suggest two engaging and informative activities that you feel will help children reduce screen time and boost their brain development and explain how.

<u>PROFESSION</u>: ADOPT SUSTAINABLE FARMING METHODS TO BOOST YOUR EARNING !!!

Natural or organic farming has suddenly gained prominence in recent years. This type of farming involves using environment-friendly and sustainable farming methods.

The farmers cultivate organic, nutritious produce without using massive quantities of fertiliser or pesticides. Crop planning, soil management, natural pest control, and marketing naturally grown food are among their duties.

Skills: Pursuing natural or organic farming does not require a formal education. However, to gain thorough knowledge on this subject, one can opt for a certificate in organic farming from IGNOU or pursue online courses on sustainable agricultural production. A bachelor's degree in agroecology is another option for individuals who want to learn about organic farming in depth.

The top universities to study agroecology in India and abroad are:
1. Punjab Agricultural University
2. University of Agricultural Sciences, Bagalkot, Karnataka
3. Wageningen University & Research, Netherlands
4. Swedish University of Agricultural Sciences

Salary: The most recent research indicates that salaries in organic or natural farming differ depending on the position. Nonetheless, in India, the minimum yearly compensation for those involved in this sector is between Rs 4 lakh and Rs 6 lakh.

+ GENERAL KNOWLEDGE +

Which is the world's smallest reptile?

A. *Brookesia minima*
B. *Brookesia nana*
C. *Lygodactylus*
D. *Rhampholeon*

OCTOBER

BMW'S ALL-NEW ELECTRIC TWO-WHEELER LAUNCHED AT RS 4.5 LAKH IN INDIA

Developed in Germany, BMW Motorrad's CE-02 will be manufactured by TVS Motor Company in Hosur, Bengaluru, as per an update received on **October 1, 2024**.

It has a maximum speed limit of 95 km/h, offers a range of 108 km, can accelerate from 0 to 50 km/h in under 3 seconds and takes more than 5 hours to charge the batteries.

It features a 3.5-inch colour TFT display, adjustable levers, smartphone connectivity, two riding modes (flow and surf), single-channel ABS, a reverse mode, single disc brakes at both ends, keyless start, automatic stability control, anti-theft alarm preparation, full-LED lighting and a USB Type-C port.

Automatic Stability Control contributes to the stability of the two-wheeler by preventing the rear wheel from spinning out of control when racing at the maximum speed.

+ GENERAL KNOWLEDGE +

Who among the following was the first Indian-born woman to go to space?

1. *Kalpana Chawla*
2. *Sunita Williams*
3. *Koneru Humpy*
4. *None of the above*

Kalpana Chawla was one of six astronauts on the Space Shuttle Columbia Mission.

Note: Born on March 17, 1962, in Karnal, Haryana, Kalpana Chawla was passionate about aircraft and flying as a child. She used to go together with her father to local flying clubs to watch the planes. Kalpana relocated to America in 1982 to chase her dream of becoming an astronaut. She received her Master's in Aerospace Engineering from the University of Texas at Arlington in 1984. She also obtained a doctorate in aerospace engineering. She joined the National Aeronautics and Space Administration in 1988. On November 19, 1997, Kalpana was launched into space for the first time. In 2003, Kalpana boarded the Space Shuttle Columbia (STS-107) with six other astronauts. All those who were aboard were killed as the Columbia blew up after re-entering the Earth's atmosphere.

VIHAA DRONE: A GAME CHANGER IN INDIAN AGRICULTURAL SECTOR

The "Vihaa" agricultural drone, which was unveiled on **October 3, 2024,** has been designed to provide a quicker and more effective method of crop management. The drone can spray fertiliser, pesticides, and other chemicals almost seven times faster than the manual approach. Farmers can thus save a significant amount of money and time by using this technology.

UAV company Amber Wings currently offers spraying services in Maharashtra, Madhya Pradesh, and Tamil Nadu and plans to expand further in the coming months.

In addition to the Vihaa agridrone, Amber Wings is developing other drone solutions, like the company's 'Atva' drone series, which has been designed for package delivery and aerial imaging and addresses the needs of logistics and e-commerce companies. Amber Wings is also developing a drone capable of carrying a 50 kg load.

Drones are unmanned aerial vehicles (UAVs) that can carry loads, fly independently or be controlled remotely by a human.

In the farming sector, drones are used for different purposes, such as insect control, crop mapping, soil analysis, and irrigation. Drones can spray crops with greater precision than a typical tractor. There is no risk of overdosing crops with pesticides because drones are programmed to spray a uniform amount of liquid in all the required regions.

HOW TO BE CREATIVE ?

Let's say Elon Musk presents you with an Optimus robot. Tell us why and how you intend to utilise it.

MAINTAIN A BALANCE BETWEEN PERSONAL AMBITIONS AND SOCIAL SENSITIVITY: PREZ MURMU TO STUDENTS

"Education is the best mode of empowerment," President Droupadi Murmu said while addressing a convocation ceremony in Rajasthan on **October 3, 2024.**

She advised students to strike a balance between their goals and social responsibility, saying that one's welfare is easily achieved by doing good to others.

Recalling Indian Constitution maker and nation builder Dr. B.R. Ambedkar's words, President Murmu noted, **"Ambedkar used to say that an educated person, who lacks education and humbleness, is more dangerous than a violent animal. I request you all that you**

should not do any such work that brings a bad name to your character. You should have integrity in all your work… You will have to maintain the spirit of the student and pave a mark of success by hard work and dedication."

CLASSICAL LANGUAGE: MARATHI, PALI, PRAKRIT, ASSAMESE AND BENGALI JOIN KANNADA AND FIVE OTHER LANGUAGES

The Union Cabinet, chaired by Prime Minister Narendra Modi, recognised Marathi, Pali, Prakrit, Assamese, and Bengali as Classical languages on **October 3, 2024.** These languages join six others that have already been recognised as classical: Tamil, Sanskrit, Telugu, Kannada, Malayalam, and Odia.

"Indian classical languages," or "Shastriya Bhasha," refers to those ancient Indian languages that have a distinct and rich literary legacy. To earn the status of 'Classical Language,' a dialect has to fulfil certain criteria. First, the early written records of the language must date back at least 1,500–2,000 years. Second, generations of speakers must view the language's ancient literature or texts as a treasured heritage. Third, the literary tradition is original and not borrowed from another speech community. Fourth, the classical language must be different from modern languages and cannot bear similarities with its later forms or branches.

INDIAN WOMEN'S TEAM BAGS SILVER AT ASIA RUGBY 7S TROPHY

Following a close 5-7 loss to the Philippines in the championship match, the Indian women's rugby team ended as runners-up in the Asia Rugby Emirates Sevens Trophy in Kathmandu.

Team India, led by Shikha Yadav, qualified at the top of their table, defeating Sri Lanka 29-10 and Indonesia 17-10. In the semis, they outshone Guam 24-7.

"A silver medal remains a commendable result for our national women's team. While Rugby India will constantly strive to turn silver into gold," said Rahul Bose, president of the Indian Rugby Football Union, on **October 6, 2024.**

The Asia Rugby Emirates Sevens Trophy, held on **October 4, 2024,** in Nepal's capital Kathmandu, featured 14 men's and 8 women's teams, representing all five sub-regions of Asia.

ON THIS DAY OF OCTOBER 25

In 1881, the spanish artist Pablo Picasso was born. He is regarded as one of the most influential artists of the 20th century.

SHORT STORY: BE READY TO STEP OUT OF YOUR COMFORT ZONE

Rajesh, a young and prosperous businessman, was travelling through a village. He remembered that his schoolmate Nilesh lived nearby and hence decided to meet him.

Rajesh was guided to Nilesh's address; it was a modest hut. When Rajesh knocked on the door, a frail-looking man opened it. When Rajesh saw Nilesh's condition, he felt sad for his friend.

Nilesh escorted his friend inside and gradually disclosed how, following a loss in his business, he was forced to sell his properties and assets to settle his debts.

Nilesh showed Rajesh a legume tree in the backyard and mentioned that he sells legumes to make ends meet. Nilesh urged Rajesh to spend the night at his place, but Rajesh was a little apprehensive, as he didn't want to burden Nilesh, but as Nilesh insisted, he agreed.

Nilesh gathered some legumes from the tree and left for the market to sell those legumes. He returned home with some rice and vegetables. After preparing the dinner, Nilesh saw that the food was sufficient to feed one person only, so he made an excuse and skipped it.

Rajesh could deduce Nilesh's intentions but couldn't do anything to convince his friend to share the food. After retiring to his room, Rajesh continued tossing on the bed, thinking about his friend, and then, in the darkest hour of the night, he picked up an axe, hacked down the legume tree, and left.

The next morning, when Nilesh saw the chopped legume tree, he was stunned. He went to call Rajesh, and when he couldn't find Rajesh in his room, he realised who was responsible for the horrible act. Everyone in the village denounced Rajesh for taking away Nilesh's sole means of support.

Six years later, Rajesh visited that village once again and was anxious to see Nilesh. When he nervously arrived at Nilesh's house, he was speechless to see that the small cottage was replaced with a large mansion.

Nilesh was happy to see Rajesh. He hugged Rajesh and said, "I have been waiting for you. I want to thank you for what you have done for me. I was furious at first, but slowly I realised why you chopped down the legume tree that night. You wanted to reduce my reliance on it."

"Had you not chopped down that tree, I would have remained dependent on it for sustenance and continued living in poverty. You helped me realise that we change, evolve and progress only if we dare to step outside our comfort zone."

SUDOKU

7	3	8					9	
			6	2				
	4					5	1	
2	1	5	4	8			6	9
	8		2	7	5	4		
3			9	6	1			
	6	3	8	5	7	9	2	4
	7	1				5	3
8		9		4	2	1	7	6

MATH PUZZLE

A.

14+19=313

25+13=328

07+15=235

10+40=. ?

B.

12 = -16,

7 = 56,

6 = -48,

1 = 08,

8 = ?

: MURLIKANT PETKAR

Padma Shri Murlikant Rajaram Petkar, India's first Paralympic gold medallist, was born on November 1, 1944, in Sangli, Maharashtra. As a child, Muralikant was deeply inspired by Khashaba Jadhav's Olympic feat in 1952; it sparked his dream of winning a medal for India

"The victory celebration was unbelievable….Taken in by the response to his win and the fervour among people, I decided there and then that I would also win a medal for my country," Petkar said.

Seven decades ago, this dream seemed unattainable in India, as there was almost no athletic infrastructure. Petkar faced societal mockery for his unconventional dreams but remained undeterred.

He started wrestling, and the more he practiced, the better his strength, technique, and reflexes got. But Petkar was forced to flee from his village after he defeated the sarpanch's (village head's) son in a bout.

Making his way to Pune, Petkar joined the Boys Battalion of the Indian Army and took up boxing. He represented the Indian Army in Tokyo, Japan, in 1964 at the International Services Sports Meet. "I won 15 fights there... a boxer from Uganda beat me in the final," Petkar disclosed.

On his return, Petkar was posted in Kashmir but his life took a drastic turn during the 1965 Indo-Pak war. He sustained nine bullet wounds and was run over by a vehicle. Although the incident left him paralysed, it couldn't dampen his determination. "Happiness was my best friend. I chose to lead a happy life. I wasn't sad or disappointed at the turn life had taken. I did not curse my destiny."

Petkar started practicing swimming in the hospital's pool and went on to compete in many international events from 1968 to 1982. However, the crowning moment came when Petkar became India's first athlete to win gold in the 50m freestyle swimming at the 1972 Heidelberg Paralympics, setting a world record (37.33 seconds).

In 2018, the Indian government honoured Petkar with the Padma Shri. "Chandu Champion," a movie based on Petkar's life featuring Kartik Aaryan in the titular role, was released in 2024.

"FUTURE IS AUTONOMOUS" SAYS ELON MUSK AS TESLA UNVEILS FIRST CYBERCAB, ROBOVAN, ROBOT

Tesla is developing the multitasking Optimus robot, which, Musk claimed, "will basically do anything you want." He clarified Optimus could serve as a teacher and friend and also take care of pets, kids, and lawns. During the event, held on **October 11, 2024**, a demo video showed Optimus carrying out household chores, including cleaning the kitchen, putting groceries away, and watering plants.

The Optimus humanoid robot may cost between $20,000 and $30,000.

The company also launched self-driving cars—Cybercabs that operate without a steering wheel or pedals and are designed to carry passengers independently.

The vehicle will go into production in 2026 and be priced at around $30,000. With only $0.20 per mile, Cybercabs' running cost will be far less than regular taxis. [1$ = Rs 85.50 (as of Dec 31, 2024); 1 mile = 1.6 km]

"You're just sitting in a comfortable little lounge, and you can do whatever you want while you're in this comfortable little lounge, and when you get out, you will be at your destination," Musk stated at the event.

The company also presented a brand-new Robovan, which can carry goods or transport 20 passengers. The vans are expected to provide fast and independent delivery, simplify logistics, and lower shipping expenses.

Tesla's autonomous (self-driving) cars will be "ten to twenty times safer" than regular cars; they will rely on AI and cameras and be charged wirelessly.

+ *DRAW WITH US* +

SAHARA DESERT WITNESSED FIRST FLOOD IN 50 YEARS

Torrential rainfall in southeast Morocco flooded portions of the Sahara Desert. The town of Tagounite, 450 km south of Rabat, the Moroccan capital, experienced almost 100 millimetres of rain in a single day in September, according to a meteorological office update received on **October 12, 2024**. Morocco is one of the most drought-prone nations in the world. NASA satellite images showed that Lake Iriqui, a dry lake bed between Tata and Zagora that had been barren for over five decades, was full of water after the rainfall.

The torrential (heavy) rain was attributed to an extratropical cyclone, which is rare for this area and could signal more extreme weather in the future.

The Sahara Desert is the world's largest hot desert and stretches over 90 lakh square kilometres across North, Central, and West Africa.

+ PROVERBS AND PHRASES+

'Make a long story short'

Meaning: *Tell something briefly.*
Example: *To make a long story short, Ravi got stuck in a traffic jam and missed his flight.*

1. I was popularly known as the "Human Computer.".

2. My talent earned me a place in the 1982 edition of the Guinness Book of World Records. However, the certificate for the record was given posthumously.

3. I took 28 seconds to answer the multiplication of two 13-digit numbers: 7,686,369,774,870 × 2,465,099,745,779; these numbers were picked randomly by the Department of Computing at Imperial College London.

4. A film based on my life was announced in May 2019; it had Vidya Balan in the title role.

DAUGHTER OF FRUIT SELLER IN BIHAR BECOMES BSF CONSTABLE

Riya Kumari, the daughter of a fruit seller from Amarpur, Bihar, secured the constable's position in the Border Security Forces (BSF) on her first attempt.

"My father worked very hard to educate me. Even in harsh weather, under the sun and rain, he continued running our fruit shop to ensure I could study," said Riya on **October 14, 2024.**

Riya, currently pursuing graduation, said her journey to success was filled with financial difficulties and other challenges, but her family's unwavering support helped her achieve her

goal.

The Border Security Force (BSF) is in charge of guarding India's borders with Bangladesh and Pakistan.

ASIAN KICKBOXING CHAMPIONSHIP: INDIA'S SHRADDHA WINS TWO GOLDS & TWO SILVERS

On **October 15**, Shraddha Rangarh became the first Indian to win multiple medals (two gold and two silver) at the Asian Kickboxing Championship 2024. Reflecting on her historic achievement, Rangarh said, "I can't even express the thrill and chills I felt.

Every time I stepped onto the tatami, I had only one thing in my mind: win for India, win for India."

The Asian Kickboxing Championships 2024 was held in Cambodia from October 8–13. 600 athletes from 23 countries participated in the event. Uzbekistan topped the medal table, with 20 gold, 5 silver, and 3 bronze, followed by Kazakhstan and Vietnam.

Kickboxing is a full-contact martial art that blends karate and boxing techniques. It involves punches and kicks at four contact points. The fighters are allowed to kick with their bare feet.

PM MODI HONOURS THE FEARLESS 'BLACK CATS' ON NSG'S 40TH ANNIVERSARY

"India salutes all NSG personnel for their unwavering dedication, courage and determination in safeguarding our nation," Prime Minister Narendra Modi wished National Security Guard (NSG) personnel on NSG's 40th Raising Day on **October 16, 2024.**

India's counterterrorism organisation, the National Security Guard, also known as the 'Black Cats,' was established on October 16, 1984, following Operation Blue Star, which was launched to drive Sikh extremists out of Amritsar's Golden Temple. The successful operation demonstrated India's need for a specialised counterterrorism unit.

To be qualified to become an NSG commando, a candidate must be under 35 years old and have at least three years of experience in the Indian army or five years in the police force.

IRONMAN 70.3 TRIATHLON EVENT ENDS IN GOA

The fourth edition of the IRONMAN 70.3 event, **a triathlon challenge that comprises 1.9 km of swimming, 90 km of cycling, and 21.1 km of running,** was flagged off at Goa's Miramar Beach on **October 27.** The Indian Army's Bishworjit Singh Saikhom qualified for the 2025 Ironman 70.3 World Championship, which will take place in Spain, after finishing first in the Ironman 70.3 triathlon event. The 34-year-old clocked an impressive 4 hr: 32 min: 04 sec to clinch gold ahead of Spain's Joaquin Berral (4:48:09). Egypt's Ahmed Iraky was placed third (4:49:10).

IRONMAN 70.3 Goa had nearly 1,200 participants from over 57 countries. All physically fit individuals can register online via the World Triathlon Corporation website or the event's dedicated website.

DON'T TRASH IT; LEARN TO FIX IT! INTERNATIONAL REPAIR DAY OBSERVED IN BENGALURU

International Repair Day is observed annually on the third Saturday in October.

On the occasion of International Repair Day 2024 (**October 19**), the city-based organisation Saahas organised a campaign in Bengaluru under the name "Repair Maadi Bengaluru" to spread the notion "Why throw when you can repair it?" by urging people to adopt sustainable habits by fixing and reusing things like toys and clothing rather than throwing them away.

About 600 people attended the all-day workshop and learnt how to fix basic electronic items like

laptops, electric kettles, headsets, etc.; stitch clothes; clean clogged taps; fix bicycles, etc. A Saahas team member highlighted how people have shifted from the old custom of repairing things to dumping goods due to the high cost of repairs.

Repairing things, she explained, is not just an affordable and environment-friendly practice but also increases a product's lifespan and supports workers like tailors and cobblers.

To help in this mission, the Indian government also established the 'Right to Repair' framework, which enables consumers to learn how to mend existing objects at an affordable rate instead of buying new ones. In addition to supporting small repair businesses, this lessens electrical waste, or "e-waste." Industries like automobiles and auto equipment, consumer durables, mobile phones and tablets, and farming equipment come under this framework.

+ POPULAR PROVERBS & PHRASES +

'When pigs fly'

Meaning: *Refers to something that is highly unlikely to happen.*
Example: *"I've already told you; I will learn to dance when pigs can fly," said Ravi.*

ROLE PLAY - VOCABULARY

Student 1: Hey! Did you read about the latest development at Tesla?

Student 2: No, I barely have any spare time to flip through the newspaper daily.

Student 1: Oh, what keeps you busy throughout the day? After school, you can devote around ten minutes to read The Newspotent. To stay informed, reading a physical newspaper is obligatory, plus The Newspotent is customised to fit the needs of the learners.

Student 2: I completely concur. However, I rarely have time for other pursuits because I have tutorials to attend, assignments to complete, etc.

Student 1: I can't specify how and when you can take some time out to read a newspaper. But I can vouch that reading a newspaper will always give you an edge over others.

Student 2: Yeah, true; I will consider your advice and start reading the newspaper regularly.

Dictionary

Obligatory: *Absolutely essential*
Concur: *To agree*
Pursuit: *An activity that you spend time doing,*
Vouch: *To testify to the truth of something*
Edge over: *To be slightly better than someone*

ON THIS DAY OF OCTOBER 21

In 1833, Swedish Chemist and Industrialist Alfred Nobel was born. The inventor of Dynamite donated his wealth to the foundation of the Nobel Prizes.

HOW TO BE CREATIVE ?

Tell us what kind of fitness activities you take part in at your school and how they have benefitted you.

NOVEMBER

EDIT

INSPIRATION: MEDICINE BABA

In Delhi, an 85-year-old man can be seen walking through neighbourhoods, knocking on doors, and asking a simple question: "Do you have any spare medicines?"

This daily mission isn't for personal gain but to help those who cannot afford costly medicines. With determination and a heart full of kindness, Delhi's 'Medicine Baba' has been gathering and distributing free medicines for over a decade, thus touching countless lives in the city. But who is this person, and why has he dedicated his life to this cause?

Omkar Nath Sharma started this mission in 2008 after the tragic incident of the Delhi Metro bridge collapse that left a deep mark on his life. The incident injured many and claimed two lives.

Sharma witnessed how some injured were sent home with minimal treatment due to high medical costs, and it was a turning point for him.

Resolved to make a difference, he began collecting unused medicines from people who no longer needed them. With a humble approach, he goes door-to-door in a simple orange kurta, spreading awareness and gathering life-saving medications. Through his dedicated efforts, he now distributes nearly Rs. 5-6 lakh worth of medications each month to those in need, walking around 5-7 km every day in the streets of Delhi.

"Leftover medicines should be donated, not discarded. I have only one dream, that the poor should have a medicine bank of their own," said Sharma.

+ PROVERBS & PHRASES +

'Turn turtle'

Meaning: *Turn upside down.*

Example: *When the truck collided, the car turned turtle.*

<u>WANDERLUST</u>: EMBARK ON AN UNFORGETTABLE JOURNEY TO A SIMPLE YET SOPHISTICATED SINGAPORE !!!

Singapore is a city-state where modern life effortlessly mingles with rich cultural heritage. The diversity of Singapore's attractions offers something for everyone—nature lovers, food enthusiasts, history buffs, and shopaholics!

Top places to visit in Singapore

Marina Bay Sands: This high-end resort has an infinity pool and observation deck offering panoramic city views. The complex has a high-end shopping mall and a science museum.

Gardens by the Bay: It is a futuristic nature park, with attractions like the 50-meter-tall Supertree Grove and the Cloud Forest, a misty dome with an indoor waterfall reaching most parts of the structures and innumerable potted exotic plants. Don't miss the Garden Rhapsody light show.

Merlion Park: Located in the heart of Singapore, this place features the well-known half-lion, half-fish monument. The best time to visit is in the evening. The Merlion's fish-shaped body symbolises Singapore's origin from 'Temasek,' a fishing settlement that got its name from the Malay word 'tasek,' meaning 'lake.'

Singaporean Cuisine: Singapore offers a variety of delicious cuisines. Must-try dishes include Hainanese Rice tossed with vegetables, Vegetarian Laksa with coconut curry broth, and Chwee Kueh, steamed rice cakes topped with radish. Don't miss Rojak, a tangy fruit and vegetable salad with sweet sauce.

Best Time to Travel: Singapore is generally an all-year destination, but if you prefer pleasant weather and fewer crowds, February to April is the best slot. These months have very little rainfall and lower temperatures and, hence, are perfect for outdoor activities.

Travel Cost: Flight tickets can cost around INR 15,000 to INR 30,000. Accommodations at any mid-range hotel can cost INR 5,000 to INR 10,000 per night, while a stay at a luxury hotel starts at INR 15,000 per night.

1 Singapore Dollar (SGD) is traded for 62.80 Indian Rupees (INR) roughly (as of Dec 31, 2024).

In Singapore, a 1.5-litre water bottle can cost around 1.85 Singapore dollars, roughly Rs. 116. Therefore, do not waste drinking water.

POETRY IS NOT ABOUT FULL STOPS BUT COMMAS: ARUNDHATHI SUBRAMANIAM

Sahitya Akademi-winning poet Arundhathi Subramaniam on **November 10** said that there is a time in everyone's life, probably in their teens, when most people are first drawn to poetry—they adore the sound of it and the music it holds, the rhyme that it offers—but it is only later that they begin to think of it as a means of self-expression.

Poet Arundhathi Subramaniam insists that "poetry can be deeply political but that does not mean one has to shout. It does not have to be strident (harsh)...

You know life is unruly, messy, vibrant, and complex, and if you're able to distil (filter) a moment in that vibrancy, in that seeming chaos..... you have succeeded."

PM MODI HAILS PANKAJ ADVANI'S 'PHENOMENAL ACCOMPLISHMENT' IN WORLD BILLIARDS CHAMPIONSHIPS

Pankaj Advani clinched his 28th World Championship title (his 20th in billiards) at the IBSF World Billiards (150-Up) 2024 on **November 10,** defeating England's Robert Hall 4-2 in the final. He became the World Billiards Champion for the 20th time.

In the semifinal, Advani had beaten his countryman Sourav Kothari 4-2.

The 39-year-old Advani is the only person to have won the Asian and World Championships in all formats of billiards and snooker.

Moreover, he has the highest number of IBSF world championships in billiards and snooker. [IBSF: International Billiards and Snooker Federation]

Snooker and billiards differ in terms of the number of balls used; while snooker uses 22 balls, billiards uses 3.

+ MATH PUZZLE +

Look at this series: 7, 10, 8, 11, 9, 12, ... What number should come next?

KARNATAKA DOCTORS CONDUCT BRAIN SURGERY ON GUITAR-PLAYING US MUSICIAN

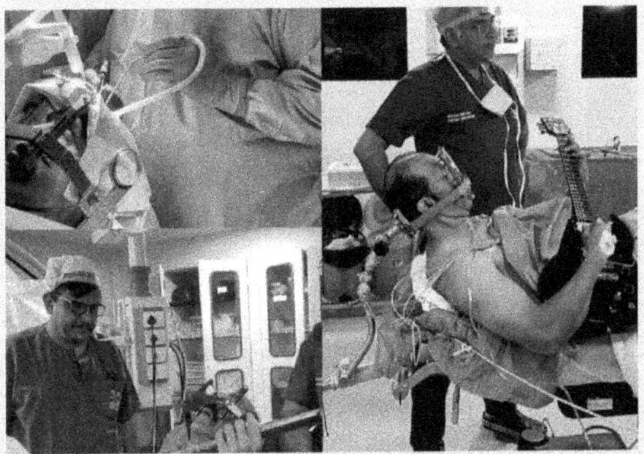

The doctors from a renowned hospital in Bengaluru successfully performed an awake brain surgery on a 65-year-old guitarist from Los Angeles, United States, who was suffering from "guitarist's dystonia," for which there is no known cure, on **November 16, 2024.**

A guitarist's dystonia, often referred to as a **musician's dystonia, is a neurological condition that results in tremors and/or involuntary muscular contractions when playing a musical instrument.**

Joseph D'Souza developed this issue on his left hand's ring and pinky fingers. The fingers would curl into his palm uncontrollably, making it difficult for him to play guitar.

The doctors performed a Vo Thalamotomy using RF (Radio Frequency) current. This means 'burning' the problematic circuit inside the brain to treat movement disorders.

This live surgery involved the patient staying awake through the 7 hours of surgery.

SUDOKU

5			4	6	7	3		9
9		3	8	1		4	2	7
1	7	4	2		3			
2	3	1	9	7	6	8	5	4
8	5	7	1	2	4		9	
4	9	6	3		8	1	7	2
				8	9	2	6	
7	8	2	6	4	1			5
	1					7		8

MATH PUZZLE

A.
[13/4÷{5/4-1/2(5/2-1/12)}]

B.
3, 2, 4 = 10
4, 3, 5 = 17
5, 4, 6 = 26
6, 5, 7 = 37
7, 6, 8 = ?

INSPIRATION: SUBHASHINI MISTRY

Subhashini Mistry is a remarkable woman whose life exemplifies the strength of kindness and perseverance.

From selling vegetables to founding Humanity Hospital in West Bengal, India, she has worked tirelessly to provide medical care to those who cannot afford it. Her journey began with a deep personal loss that inspired her to make sure others wouldn't face the same tragedy.

"Where there is a will, there is a way"

Born into an underprivileged family during the Bengal Famine, Subhashini Mistry's life started with hardship. By the age of 12, she was married to an agricultural labourer and struggled hard to make ends meet.

In 1971, she endured a greater tragedy when her husband started complaining of abdominal discomfort and was rushed to a government hospital. Even though the government hospital was required to treat the poor for free, only those with resources or power received medical attention.

A lack of timely treatment claimed her husband's life.

Although death ended her husband's torment, it left Subhashini in deep shock as the sole breadwinner of the family was gone, and she was left with 4 hungry mouths to feed.

Following the premature demise of her husband, Subhashini committed herself to constructing a hospital for the underprivileged so that no one would have to endure the same suffering as she had.

Subhashini began her journey towards building the hospital by taking up different odd jobs, from roof polishing to house cleaning. While her other three children assisted her in her work, she sent her son Ajoy, who was an excellent student, to an orphanage to finish his schooling. She eventually began selling vegetables and saved most of her earnings. She spent twenty years slogging tirelessly and saving every penny possible.

Subhashini purchased an acre of property in her husband's hometown in 1992, thus laying the cornerstone of the Humanity Hospital. She was able to erect a modest structure with the bare necessities for medical care with the help of local people, who provided labour, raw materials, and also donated cash.

Only a few people know that for many years, even after 'Humanity Hospital' was established, Subhashini continued selling vegetables. She didn't live in a fancy house or wear expensive clothes; instead, she invested all her savings into expanding the hospital and upgrading its facilities. She only consented to stop selling vegetables after her son, Ajoy, who went on to become a doctor, pressed her.

Achievements:

Since its inception, the facility has expanded to 9,000 square feet and now houses multiple departments, including cardiology, oncology, and gynaecology. Here, the underprivileged receive free treatment, while others pay a nominal fee of Rs. 10 to help with operating expenses.

In 2009, Subhashini Mistry was presented with the 'Godfrey Phillips Award' for her humanitarian efforts. She also received the 'Women Transforming India Award' in 2017 and in 2018, Subhashini was felicitated with India's fourth-highest civilian award, the 'Padma Shri,' in recognition of her social work.

ON THIS DAY OF NOVEMBER 25 :

In 2020, Argentine football star Diego Maradona passed away. He was named the top player of the 20th century by FIFA.

MULTI-CULTURAL: PHILIPPINES' RIGID SHOE CODE FOR DRIVING

Driving in flip-flops might seem harmless and comfortable in the sweltering heat of tropical countries, but in the Philippines, it can invite legal trouble for the driver.

According to Philippine traffic law, wearing improper footwear while driving, such as flip-flops or sandals, is considered unsafe and may result in penalties if one violates the rule.

Are you wondering why such laws have been framed?

Let us explain. The rationale behind this regulation is that flip-flops don't provide adequate grip and can easily slip off, potentially causing drivers to lose control of the vehicle, particularly during emergencies when quick and precise pedal control is important.

To promote road safety, the Land Transport Office in the Philippines has warned about the need to wear suitable driving shoes that have a strong grip and securely cover one's foot. If law enforcement authorities feel that a driver's footwear compromises safety, they have the authority to stop them.

Hence, while driving in the Philippines, wear suitable footwear, as this will not just lower the chance of a mishap but also improve your control over the car and make driving a smooth experience.

NCC INSTILS DISCIPLINE, LEADERSHIP, SERVICE IN YOUTH: 'PM MODI ON MANN KI BAAT'

Prime Minister Narendra Modi emphasised the need to be associated with the National Cadet Corps (NCC) in his monthly radio talk show 'Mann Ki Baat' on **November 24, 2024.** "NCC instils (infuses) discipline, leadership and service in youth," PM Modi said. Over 5000 schools and colleges are part of NCC. **Founded in 1948, the NCC is the youth wing of the Indian Armed Forces. National Cadet Corps Day is celebrated on the** **fourth Sunday of November.**

Addressing the nation's declining sparrow population, PM Modi stated that special measures are being taken to conserve the bird. **He praised the Kudugal Trust in Chennai, which trains children to construct small wooden sparrow homes. They have made 10,000 of these nests in the past four years.** A Mysuru-based organisation has launched the 'Early Bird' campaign and operates a library to educate kids about different birds.

He next stressed the success of the 'Ek Ped Maa Ke Naam' campaign, stating that the nation has planted almost 100 crore trees in 5 months.

+ HOW TO BE CREATIVE ? +

What modification or enhancement would you have suggested to better the lives of children throughout the world if you had been allowed to become the Chief of UNICEF for a day?

CABINET APPROVES 'NATIONAL MISSION ON NATURAL FARMING'

"Natural farming" is a chemical-free traditional farming method. It avoids the use of synthetic fertilisers, pesticides, and heavy machinery. Natural farming practices focus on manufacturing agricultural inputs like fertilisers on the farm using dung and urine of cows and on-farm-made botanical extracts. These agricultural practices support soil health and biodiversity.

The Union Cabinet, on **November 26, 2024,** approved the launch to promote natural farming practices for providing safe and nutritious food for all. The mission aims to support farmers in reducing their dependency on externally purchased inputs like pesticides or fertilisers.

The National Mission on Natural Farming (NMNF) is focused on scientifically reviving and strengthening agricultural practices towards sustainability and climate resilience (the capacity to withstand adverse weather).

"The National Mission on Natural Farming... marks a transformative shift in Indian agriculture. Through this effort, we are nurturing soil health, protecting biodiversity, and securing our agricultural future," said Prime Minister Narendra Modi.

+ DRAW WITH US +

HOW TO BE CREATIVE ?

Mention what advantages of natural farming you will highlight while attempting to popularise the concept in your locality.

LONGEST-LIVING BIRD CARNABY'S COCKATOO CAN SURVIVE 35 YEARS IN WILD

Carnaby's cockatoo, an endangered large black cockatoo found only in southwest Australia, is among the longest-living bird species in the world, living up to 35 years in the wild,

according to new research published on **November 28, 2024.**

The oldest bird, a male born in 1986, was photographed by researchers in 2021 as it was identified by a leg band fitted in November 1986.

The research team studied five females and three males, discovering that their ages ranged from 21 to 35 years, confirming their remarkable longevity.

ON THIS DAY OF NOVEMBER 04 :

In 1957, the Soviet Union launched Sputnik 2, which carried the dog Laika, the first living creature to be shot into space and orbit Earth.

AUSTRALIA BECOMES THE FIRST NATION TO BAN SOCIAL MEDIA FOR THOSE UNDER 16

Australia made history by becoming the first country in the world to impose a nationwide ban on social media platforms (TikTok, Facebook, Snapchat, Reddit, X and Instagram) for children under 16.

The Australian Parliament approved this historic law on **November 28, 2024.**

The law aims to protect the mental health and general well-being of youth from the negative effects of excessive internet use.

According to the law enacted by the Australian Senate, social media companies, including Facebook, Instagram, etc., face fines of up to Australian $50 million if they don't stop minors

under 16 from creating accounts. YouTube, however, is exempt from the prohibition. [1 million = 10 lakh;

1 Australian dollar = Rs. 53 (as of Dec 31, 2024)]

CENTRE DECLARES SNAKEBITES A NOTIFIABLE DISEASE IN INDIA

As per data received from the Ministry of Health and Family Welfare on **November 29, 2024,** around 50,000 deaths in India occur due to an estimated 30-40 lakh snakebites annually. This accounts for half of all snakebite deaths globally.

"Snakebites are an issue of public health and in certain cases, they cause mortality (death), morbidity (suffering), and disability. Farmers, tribal populations, etc. are at higher risk," said Union Health Secretary Punya Salila Srivastava.

The common krait, Indian cobra, Russell's viper, and saw-scaled viper are responsible for about 90 percent of snakebites in India.

Although 80 percent of cases may be treated with polyvalent anti-snake venom (ASV), the lack of healthcare facilities and skilled personnel to treat snakebite victims is still a problem.

However, Srivastava said the Centre has set a target to "halve the snakebite-related deaths by 2030. "

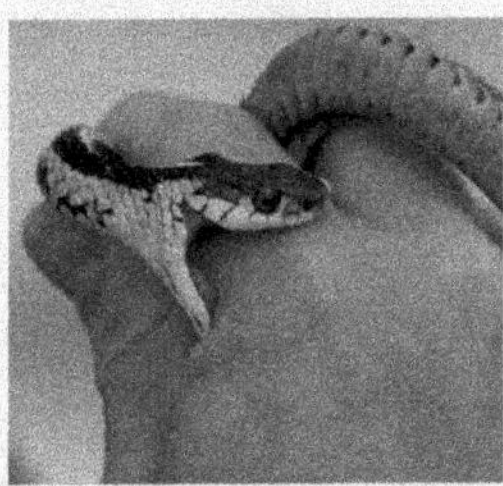

WHO AM I ?

1. I am an Argentine professional footballer widely regarded as one of the greatest players of all time and have won a record eight Ballon d'Or awards and six European Golden Shoes.

2. I was named the world's best player by FIFA.

3. I am the most decorated player in the history of professional football having won 45 team trophies, including twelve league titles, four UEFA Champions Leagues, two Copa Américas, and one FIFA World Cup.

4. I founded a non-profit organisation in 2007 with the goal of protecting the health and safety of young children globally.

+ HOW TO BE CREATIVE ? +

List one change you hope to see in your state by the end of the year that will help guide its progress.

WHY MUST YOU BE AWARE OF CPR TECHNIQUES?

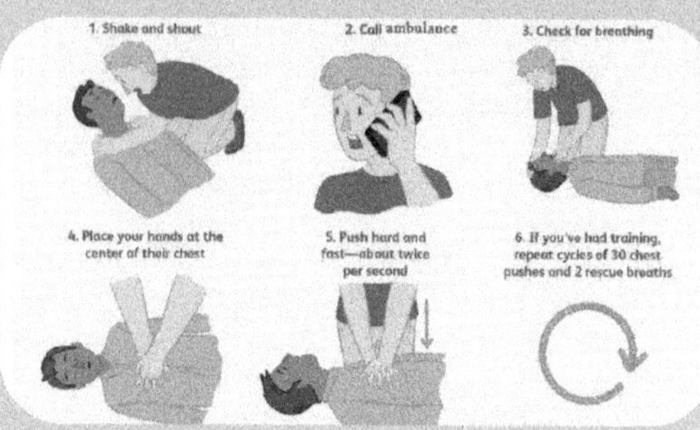

In 2023, the rising incidence of heart attacks and sudden cardiac arrests persisted as individuals who didn't show any warning signs heretofore passed away while engaging in supposedly harmless activities like jogging or training at gyms. Experts estimate that cardiac arrest accounts for almost 12 lakh deaths among youngsters in India, and this number has only gone up in the last few years.

What is CPR?

When a person's heart stops beating, cardiopulmonary resuscitation, or CPR, is an emergency procedure employed to save lives. Immediate CPR after cardiac arrest can double or triple the likelihood of survival.

CPR can maintain the flow of oxygen-rich blood to the brain and other organs until emergency medical assistance arrives.

The body stops receiving oxygen-rich blood when the heart stops beating, and in barely a few minutes, brain damage might occur due to its shortage.

How is CPR performed?

There are two well-recognised forms of CPR:

1. Traditional CPR with chest compressions and mouth-to-mouth breathing at a ratio of 30:2 compressions to breaths is recommended for medical professionals and individuals with training. It is standard for paramedics to perform chest compressions on adult cardiac arrest victims at a rate of 100 to 120 per minute, to a minimum depth of 2 inches (5 cm), but not deeper than 2.4 inches [6 cm].

2. You should perform hands-on CPR if you lack CPR training or are afraid to give rescue breaths. This entails continuously performing 100 to 120 chest compressions per minute until paramedics arrive. But before starting with CPR, make sure you seek medical help over the call.

It's always preferable to try CPR rather than doing nothing at all. Remember that the difference between taking action and doing nothing might cost someone their life.

DECEMBER

EDIT

18-YEAR-OLD KARNATAKA GIRL AMONG YOUNGEST INDIANS TO OBTAIN COMMERCIAL PILOT LICENSE

18-year-old Samaira Hullur of Vijayapura, Karnataka, made history on **December 2, 2024,** by possibly becoming the youngest Indian to obtain a Commercial Pilot License (CPL). "Now, I am the youngest commercial pilot in the country," claimed Samaira.

Samaira completed the six mandatory courses at Vinod Yadav Aviation Academy, which included flying a light aircraft and gaining 200 hours of flying experience, to become eligible for CPL.

She credits her success to her mentor, Captain Tapesh Kumar, who became India's youngest captain at the age of 25.

CPL is a license to fly multi-engine aircraft and work as a professional pilot, either as a commercial airline pilot or as a private charter pilot. To obtain a CPL in India, an aspirant must have passed class 12 with physics, chemistry, and mathematics.

+ GENERAL KNOWLEDGE +

Which country has the highest concentration of elephants in the world?

1. *India*
2. *Botswana*
3. *Nairobi*
4. *Algeria*

Botswana is a landlocked country in Southern Africa.

Note: Botswana is home to the world's largest population of African elephants, estimated at around 130,000. This accounts for nearly one-third of Africa's total elephant population. The highest concentration of elephants is in the Chobe National Park and Linyanti region. Botswana houses the African savanna elephant (Loxodonta africana), the largest elephant species and the largest terrestrial mammal on Earth. They are easily distinguished by their large ears—which allow them to radiate excess heat—and front legs, which are noticeably longer than the hind legs. With 29,964 elephants, India has the largest number of wild Asian elephants. Karnataka has the highest elephant population in India, with 6,395 elephants.

MEN'S HOCKEY JUNIOR ASIA CUP 2024: INDIA BEATS PAKISTAN 5-3 TO BAG THE TITLE FOR RECORD-BREAKING 5TH TIME

The Indian hockey team triumphed over their arch-rivals, Pakistan, 5-3, in the Men's Junior Asia Cup 2024 hockey final in Muscat, Oman, on **December 4, 2024.** With four goals, Araijeet Singh Hundal was the winning team's hero, while Dilraj Singh scored one goal.

Although Pakistan took an early lead in the game, Araijeet helped India bounce back within a minute by levelling the scores.

Hannan Shahid scored one goal, and Sufyan Khan struck two for Pakistan.

The most successful team in the tournament's history is India, with five titles, followed by Pakistan, with three.

PM Modi congratulated the winning team, praising their unmatched skill, determination and teamwork.

"I WANT CRICKETERS TO EDUCATE THEMSELVES," SAYS IPL'S COSTLIEST ALL-ROUNDER VENKATESH IYER

India all-rounder Venkatesh Iyer thinks that education is important and should be pursued alongside cricket. The batter, on **December 9, 2024,** shared that he has been pursuing a PhD in finance and that **by the time the IPL begins, his name will have the prefix "Dr." before it.**

Iyer, who recently became the fourth-costliest pick in the history of the IPL after he was picked by Kolkata Knight Riders (KKR) for INR 23.75 crore, said, **"Education will stay with you till you die; a cricketer cannot play till 60."**

Venkatesh Iyer obtained an offer from Deloitte in 2018 following the completion of his MBA in Finance. However, he chose not to accept it and concentrate on his cricket career.

"If you (cricketers) can complete your graduation or post-graduation, you definitely should," Venkatesh said.

PROFESSION: MAKE A LIVING BY MONITORING FOOD QUALITY!!!

Job Title: *Food Inspector*

Job description: *A food inspector is responsible for ensuring that food products meet health standards and are safe and suitable for consumption.*

Responsibilities: Food inspectors regularly visit food processing plants, restaurants, grocery stores, etc., to check for cleanliness, proper food handling, pest control, and compliance with safety protocols. They collect samples of food products to test for bacteria, pesticides, chemical residues, and other contaminants to ensure that foods are safe to consume and the additives are within permissible limits.

Educational Qualification: To succeed in this industry, one must hold a bachelor's degree in biotechnology, food technology, biochemistry, or related disciplines. Students between 21–40 years of age and willing to become food inspectors must pass the Food Safety Officer (FSO) exam conducted by the Food Safety and Authority of India (FSSAI). The FSSAI regulates the production, import, distribution, storage, and sale of food. It also is in charge of establishing food safety standards.

The top universities to study Food Science in India are:

- Padmashree Institute of Management and Sciences, Bengaluru;
- Amity University, Noida.

Salary: The average salary of an entry-level food inspector is around Rs 35,000 to Rs 40,000 per month.

+ PROVERBS & PHRASES +

The Benefit of the Doubt

Meaning: *To choose to think positively about someone despite having doubts.*

Example: *"Ramesh didn't know whether Anil's story was true or not, but he decided to give Anil the benefit of the doubt".*

GOOGLE TO TIE UP WITH NCERT, LAUNCH YOUTUBE CHANNELS IN 29 INDIAN LANGUAGES

On **December 12, 2024,** tech giant Google announced a partnership with the National Council of Educational Research and Training (NCERT) to bring quality education to far corners of India.

In the upcoming months, NCERT will launch different YouTube channels that align with the syllabus for grades 1–12.
The channels will empower teachers, parents, and students nationwide by providing educational information in interesting and easily accessible formats in 29 Indian languages, including Indian Sign Language.
The Google-owned YouTube first rolled out courses in India in 2022 to help creators offer a structured learning experience. In 2024, the company focused on empowering even more creators to develop and share courses, enabling them to reach wider audiences and increase their impact on learners.

Further, to help understand, it has taken it a step further with the roll-out of "Key Concepts.".
"Using AI, we identify concepts covered in a video and may provide definitions from the web of those concepts across subjects like biology, physics, and chemistry," said YouTube Learning's spokesperson.

The online video-sharing platform has also introduced quizzes to help learners apply what they've learnt. Its YouTube Player for Education is a product designed for learners that improves the way YouTube videos are shown in popular educational tools.

ON THIS DAY OF DECEMBER 04:

In 1996, the unmanned space vehicle Mars Pathfinder was launched from Cape Canaveral, Florida, in order to explore the surface of Mars.

INSPIRATION: KIRAN BEDI

Imagine a young police officer dragging away a car belonging to the Prime Minister's office because it was parked illegally. While most people would think twice, the courageous Kiran Bedi didn't hesitate. This bold act earned her the nickname "Crane Bedi" and showed her commitment to doing what's right.

As India's first woman IPS (Indian Police Service) officer, she broke barriers and changed how people saw women in the police force.

Rise of Kiran Bedi

Born on June 9, 1949, in Amritsar, Kiran Bedi's journey is one of determination and courage. Before joining the IPS, Kiran Bedi was an accomplished

tennis player and won several national and state championships, including the Asian Lawn Tennis Championship, in 1972.

Bedi's educational qualification was equally impressive—she earned a PhD in social sciences and degrees in law and political science, preparing herself to make a difference in the world. Even during her college days, Bedi never shied away from

protesting against injustices and questioned unjust procedures. This fearless streak only grew stronger when she joined the IPS. While serving as a traffic police officer in Delhi, she introduced several traffic reforms, including "traffic parks," to educate children about road safety. She was also instrumental in managing the traffic during the 1982 Asian Games, which brought her immense praise.

In the early years of her service, she even volunteered to clean drains during a cholera outbreak in Delhi. Kiran Bedi became the first Indian woman to head the United Nations Civil Police unit during UN peacekeeping operations.

Achievements

Kiran Bedi's life is full of fascinating and inspiring stories. One of Bedi's most recognised contributions was transforming Tihar Jail. While serving as the "Head of the Prison," Bedi introduced initiatives such as yoga, education, and skill development, allowing the inmates to transform their lives.

This groundbreaking work earned her the UN (United Nations) Civilian Police Prize in 1994, making her the first Indian woman to receive it.

Bedi has received over 40 awards, including the prestigious Ramon Magsaysay Award (1994) for her efforts to reform prisons and her innovative administrative skills.

Kiran Bedi founded two NGOs, 'Navjyoti India Foundation' and 'India Vision Foundation,' which work on issues like education, women empowerment, etc.

Bedi has authored several books, including "I Dare!" and "It's Always Possible," where she chronicles her life and career challenges. She is also a sought-after motivational speaker.

Through her writings and speeches, Kiran Bedi continues to motivate others to uphold ethical conduct.

MIZORAM: INTERNATIONAL PARAGLIDING ACCURACY CHAMPIONSHIP & AIR SPORTS FESTIVAL CONCLUDES

The closing ceremony of the International Paragliding Accuracy Championship and Air Sports Festival 2024 was held on **December 14** in Mizoram. The championship, to promote adventure tourism, saw 30 athletes from six countries—India, Korea, Kazakhstan, Spain, Indonesia, and Nepal—compete at the event. Each category winner was awarded Rs. 2 lakh.

Mizoram's Serchhip town, with its natural beauty, stands out as one of the best locations in India for paragliding and adventure sports.

International events like the Paragliding Championship would help the people of the state to showcase the ethnicity and diversity of Mizoram to the world.

HOW TO BE CREATIVE ?

Do you believe that India should follow Australia's approach and forbid minors under 16 from using social media? Justify your claim.

WOMEN'S JUNIOR ASIA CUP HOCKEY: INDIA CROWNED CHAMPIONS, BEAT CHINA IN PENALTY SHOOTOUT

The Indian hockey team beat China 3-2 in a penalty shootout in the final of the Women's Junior Asia Cup on **December 15** to lift the title for the second time in a row.

After a 1-1 draw in regulation time, the title clash went to a shootout that saw the defending champion come out victorious.

Jinzhuang Tan (30 minutes) scored the first goal for China, but Kanika Siwach (41') equalised it for India, and the match went into a penalty shootout. Sakshi Rana, Ishika, and Sunelita Toppo scored for India in the penalty shootout, and goalkeeper Nidhi made three crucial saves to help her side lift the title.

Hockey India announced a cash prize of Rs. 2 lakhs for each player and Rs. 1 lakh for the support staff.

ON THIS DAY OF DECEMBER 20:

In 1998, French footballer Kylian Mbappe was born. He scored a hat-trick in the 2022 FIFA world cup qatar final against Argentina.

SUDOKU

MATH PUZZLE

A. The smallest number which when diminished by 7, is divisible 12, 16, 18, 21 and 28 is?

LEGENDARY TABLA MAESTRO ZAKIR HUSSAIN PASSES AWAY AT 73

Ustad Zakir Hussain, who is considered one of the greatest tabla players of all time, succumbed to heart-related issues on Sunday, **December 15.** He transformed Indian rhythm scores by introducing jazz fusion and foreign music components into the Hindustani gharana.

In 1990, Hussain was presented with the Sangeet Natak Akademi Award, and in 1999, he was awarded the United States National Endowment for the Arts' National Heritage Fellowship, the highest award given to traditional artists and musicians.

Hussain received five Grammy Awards in his career, including

three at the 66th Grammy Awards in 2024.

The legendary tabla player was felicitated with the Padma Shri (1988), the Padma Bhushan (2002), and the Padma Vibhushan (2023) in recognition of his contributions to Indian music.

RAVICHANDRAN ASHWIN ANNOUNCED RETIREMENT FROM INTERNATIONAL CRICKET

Team India all-rounder Ravichandran Ashwin, India's second-leading wicket-taker after legendary leg-spinner Anil Kumble, ended his career on **December 18, 2024,** with 537 wickets at an average of 24 in 106 Tests.

Ashwin, who made his Test debut in 2011, announced his retirement from international cricket at the end of the third Border-Gavaskar Trophy Test in Brisbane, which ended in a draw due to rain.

"I do feel there's a bit of punch left in me... and I would probably showcase that in club-level cricket," said the seventh-highest wicket-taker in Test cricket.

In Tests, Ashwin was one of the big figures in the Indian team's 12-year-long home domination and played a starring role in the 2020/21 Border-Gavaskar Trophy win in Australia. He also won a record 11 Player-of-the-Series awards, level with Muthiah Muralitharan.

JITENDRA SINGH LAUNCHES ANTI-PESTICIDE SUIT TO SAFEGUARD FARMERS' HEALTH

Union Minister of State (Independent Charge) for Earth Sciences Dr. Jitendra Singh on **December 18, 2024,** launched 'Kisan Kavach,' the first-of-its-kind anti-pesticide bodysuit, to protect farmers from the harmful effects of pesticide exposure.

The fabric of the 'Kisan Kavach' suit can deactivate pesticides upon contact through nucleophilic-mediated hydrolysis, thereby preventing pesticide-induced toxicity and lethality. The bodysuit is washable and reusable and can last up to a year. It employs advanced fabric technology to deactivate harmful pesticides upon contact, ensuring farmer safety.

While the bodysuit is priced at Rs 4,000, Singh assured that as production scales up, the suit's affordability will increase, making it accessible to more farmers nationwide.

Pesticides are used in agriculture to protect crops from pests, weeds, and diseases. **Prolonged exposure to common agricultural chemicals (agrichemicals) like insecticides, herbicides (kill weeds), fungicides (prevent the growth of fungi), rodenticides, solvents, fertilisers and veterinary chemicals can lead to various immediate or long-term health effects,** including headaches, poisoning, burns, nervous system disorders, cancers, birth defects, breathing disorders, vision loss, and, in extreme cases, death. The bodysuit is developed by BRIC-inStem, Bengaluru, in collaboration with Sepio Health.

1. I play as a forward for the Indian Super League (ISL) club Bengaluru and am the all-time top scorer in ISL history.

2. I am the fourth-highest international goalscorer. I announced my retirement from all forms of international football in June 2024.

3. I received the Arjuna Award in 2011 for my outstanding sporting achievement and the Padma Shri Award in 2019.

4. In 2021, I received the Khel Ratna Award, India's highest sporting honour, and became the first footballer to receive the award.

JYOTIRADITYA SCINDIA PRAISES MADHYA PRADESH STUDENT FOR DEVELOPING HUMAN-CARRYING DRONE

Medhansh Trivedi, a class 12 student from Madhya Pradesh's Gwalior, has developed a single-seater drone, which can carry a person weighing up to 80 kg and sustain flight for nearly six minutes.

The drone named MLDT 01 was built at a cost of Rs 3.5 lakh. It is 1.8 metres long with equal width and is currently being flown only up to a height of 10 metres for safety concerns.

Medhansh revealed that he had thought of designing this human-carrying drone after being inspired by China's drone technology.

Union Minister of Civil Aviation and Steel, Jyotiraditya Scindia, visited Medhansh on **December 20, 2024,** and encouraged him to use this innovation as a launchpad for the future. He also urged Medhansh to start preparing to study at the best universities in the world and promised all the assistance he required.

25 PERCENT OF COUNTRY'S AREA UNDER GREEN COVER: MINISTER

Total forest and tree cover in India is 8, 27,357 sq km, which is 25.17 percent of the nation's total geographical area (32, 87,263 sq km), Minister for Environment, Forest and Climate Change Bhupender Yadav said on **December 21, 2024.**

The top three states with the largest forest cover by area are Madhya Pradesh (77,073 sq km), followed by Arunachal Pradesh (65,882 sq km) and Chhattisgarh (55,812 sq km). **In Karnataka, the forest cover extends over 40,678.22 sq km,** nearly 21% of the state's total geographical area.

The top three states showing a maximum increase in forest cover are Mizoram, followed by Gujarat and Odisha.

The 'India State of Forest Report 2023' provides comprehensive data on forest cover, tree cover, mangrove cover, instances of forest fire, agroforestry, etc.

'MEDITATION NOT A LUXURY, BUT A NECESSITY': SRI SRI RAVI SHANKAR

At the inaugural session of the first-ever World Meditation Day **(December 21)** at United Nations headquarters in New York, spiritual guru Sri Sri Ravi Shankar emphasised the necessity of meditation.

"Today, meditation is not a luxury as it was thought, but it is a necessity. I would call it mental hygiene," Sri Sri Ravi Shankar said. He further explained that meditation heightens our awareness of the environment and sensitivity towards those around us.

"It helps us avoid antisocial behaviours that can harm both ourselves and others," he added. Originating in India thousands of years ago, meditation is a set of practices that are meant to promote increased awareness and focused attention.

+ PROVERBS AND PHRASES +

A recipe for disaster

Meaning: *Something is a recipe for disaster if it's going to cause trouble or serious problems.*

Example: *"Indulging in excessive screen time, skipping classes, and not studying is a recipe for disaster!" warned the teacher.*

HEALTH: NUTTY WONDER!

Nuts are a nutrient-rich food, providing fiber, protein, healthy fats, vitamins, and micronutrients like magnesium and calcium. They can lower cholesterol and triglyceride levels, reducing cardiovascular disease risk. Although calorie-dense, nuts help control hunger and support weight management due to their high protein and fiber content. They are a satisfying snack option for health-conscious individuals. Additionally, nuts are high in unsaturated fats that improve

heart health, regulate blood sugar levels, and support strong bones and teeth, helping prevent osteoporosis.

THE HERO OF KARGIL: REMEMBERING TASHI NAMGYAL'S VITAL ROLE IN VICTORY

A shepherd from Ladakh, Tashi Namgyal, created history while searching for his missing yaks in May 1999. He spotted Pakistani soldiers in Pathani attire digging bunkers atop the Batalik mountain range in early May 1999. Realising the gravity of the situation, he promptly informed the Indian Army, a timely warning that played a pivotal role in shaping India's military response and proved instrumental in India's victory.

It earned him recognition as the heroic shepherd whose alertness turned the tide of the conflict.

He would always be invited to the Kargil Vijay Diwas after 1999. He had attended the 25th Kargil Vijay Diwas earlier this year in Drass, accompanied by his daughter Tsering Dolkar, a teacher.

The Army gave a hero's farewell to Tashi Namgyal at his funeral on **December 22, 2024,**–– "Fire and Fury Corps pays tribute to Mr. Tashi Namgyal on his sudden demise. His invaluable contribution to the nation during Op Vijay 1999 shall remain etched in golden letters. We offer deep condolences to the bereaved family in this hour of grief."

Dr Edward Jenner created the world's first successful vaccine.

Note: Vaccines work by introducing a weakened or dead virus into the body. This teaches the immune system to produce memory cells and antibodies to defend against the illness. In 1796, Dr. Edward Jenner developed the world's first vaccine by using material from cowpox sores to protect people against smallpox, a deadly disease. He noticed that milkmaids who contracted cowpox (a much milder disease) did not get smallpox. This inspired him to test his theory. Using material from a cowpox blister, Jenner vaccinated James Phipps, an 8-year-old kid. Later, when exposed to smallpox, the boy did not contract the disease, supporting Jenner's notion that cowpox can serve as a protective immunisation against smallpox. Jenner's discovery led to widespread vaccination practices and, eventually, the eradication of smallpox by 1980.

RENOWNED ECONOMIST AND STATESMAN DR. MANMOHAN SINGH PASSES AWAY AT 92

Former Indian Prime Minister Dr. Manmohan Singh, 92, passed away on **December 26, 2024.** He was admitted to the All India Institute of Medical Sciences (AIIMS) in New Delhi following a decline in his health.

Dr. Singh, who earned his doctorate in Economics from Oxford University, played a pivotal role in Indian policymaking. He served in several important capacities, including as Director of the Reserve Bank of India and as the Ministry of Finance's Chief Economic Advisor.

Singh rose to national prominence as India's Finance Minister (1991-96) under the leadership of Prime Minister P.V. Narasimha Rao, where he spearheaded economic reforms that transformed India's economy.

These reforms liberalised trade, reduced governmental controls, and integrated India into the global market.

Dr. Singh was sworn in as Prime Minister on May 22, 2004, and served two consecutive terms, making him the first Prime Minister since Jawaharlal Nehru to be re-elected after completing a full five-year term.

Singh's government implemented landmark legislation in education, food security, and information technology, emphasising inclusive growth.

One of the defining achievements of his tenure was the India-US Civil Nuclear Agreement, a historic milestone in international diplomacy that opened avenues for civilian nuclear cooperation and strengthened India's foreign relations.

Additionally, Singh's government launched pivotal initiatives, including the Mahatma Gandhi National Rural Employment Guarantee Act (MGNREGA), which provided millions of rural Indians with employment opportunities and financial stability.

IMAGE DECODER

RASHTRIYA BAL PURASKAR 2024: PRESIDENT MURMU FELICITATED 17 YOUNG HEROES

The Pradhan Mantri Rashtriya Bal Puraskar is India's highest civilian honour awarded to exceptional students under the age of 18. *This prestigious recognition celebrates outstanding achievements across seven categories: art and culture, bravery, innovation, science and technology, social service, sports, and environment.*

On **December 26,** President Droupadi Murmu conferred awards to 17 remarkable children during a special ceremony held at the Rashtrapati Bhavan Cultural Centre, New Delhi. The honourees included seven boys and ten girls from 14 states and union territories. Each awardee received a medal, a certificate, and a citation booklet.

The president congratulated all award winners and said that the entire country and society are proud of them.

Saurav Kumar, aged just 9, was honoured for saving three girls from drowning, and Ioanna Thapa, 17, was lauded for rescuing 36 residents of a burning flat.

In technology, Sindhoora Raja, 15, was honoured for developing a self-stabilising device for Parkinson's patients. Meanwhile, 17-year-old Risheek Kumar, a cybersecurity entrepreneur, was recognised for founding Kashmir's first cybersecurity firm and launching the transformative "Hack Free Bharat" initiative to enhance digital safety.

Vyas Om Jignesh, a 17-year-old with cerebral palsy, was honoured for his unparalleled dedication to Sanskrit literature, having memorised over 5,000 shlokas.

The realm of sports saw incredible accomplishments: Hembati Nag, a judo player from a Naxal-affected region, was felicitated for her silver medal at the Khelo India National Games. The other recipients included 9-year-old Saanvi Sood, who captivated hearts with her record-breaking mountaineering achievements, including summiting Mount Kilimanjaro and 3-year-old Anish Sarkar, who made history as the youngest FIDE-ranked chess player and became the youngest recipient of the award.

+ HOW TO BE CREATIVE? +

If you were given a chance to nominate someone for the Rashtriya Bal Pruruskar, who would you nominate and why?

The Newspotent is more than just a newspaper—it's a student's daily guide to the world. With a sharp focus on relevant, engaging, and unbiased content, it has become the go-to newspaper for students, helping them stay informed, think critically, and grow confidently.

What is The Newspotent? It's simple —a newspaper that is entirely student-focused. No political bias, no unnecessary fluff—just pure, 100% student-relevant content. Every single article—down to the very last word— is written with exactly what a student requires for today and tomorrow.

In the last 4+ years, The Newspotent has become the go-to newspaper for students. Its success comes from a fresh and unconventional approach, coverage of news, unique writing style, good presentation, and constant ideas striving to engage and inspire students. But the results speak for themselves—out of the 50,000 handwritten reviews collected from students, teachers, principals, and even school founders, there have been no significant negative remarks. Pretty cool, isn't it?

Headquartered in Karnataka, The Newspotent has built a strong presence across cities and districts. Retaining the tag of being a Perfect Student Newspaper, it ensures students receive daily doses of news updates, helping them understand and realise how fast the world is growing. Covering news topics including regional, state, national, and international news—plus sports, science, tech, health, research, medicine, and even automobiles—The Newspotent keeps students informed and ahead.

www.ingramcontent.com/pod-product-compliance
Lightning Source LLC
Chambersburg PA
CBHW040126150726
48005CB00015B/2389